Zulu: The Truth Behind the Film

Zulu: The Truth Behind the Film

Paul Raby

© Paul Raby 2009

Published by Paul Raby 2009

All rights reserved. Reproduction of this book by photocopying or electronic means for non-commercial purposes is permitted. Otherwise, no part of this book may be reproduced, adapted, stored in a retrieval system or transmitted by any means, electronic, mechanical, photocopying, or otherwise without the prior written permission of the author.

(Extracts from) *Rorke's Drift 1879* by Ian Knight © Osprey Publishing Ltd

(Extracts from) *Nothing Remains But to Fight*, by Ian Knight, published by Greenhill Books, London, 1993. Reproduced by kind permission of the publisher.

Extracts used with kind permission of Penguin Group (UK)

(Extracts from) *Rorke's Drift* by Adrian Greaves. Reproduced by kind permission of Cassell Plc., an imprint of The Orion Publishing Group, London.
Copyright © Adrian Greaves, 2002
First published in Great Britain by Cassell in 2002

ISBN 978-0-9564301-0-6

Cover design by Clare Brayshaw

Cover image © Hongqi Zhang/Dreamstime.com

Prepared and printed by:
York Publishing Services Ltd
64 Hallfield Road
Layerthorpe
York YO31 7ZQ
Tel: 01904 431213

Website: www.yps-publishing.co.uk

INTRODUCTION

"Dwarfing the mightiest! Towering over the greatest!"

This is a famous quote from the trailer of the epic film "Zulu".

This book is dedicated to the above film and gives you personal details of the characters and historical facts about the battle, quotes from the defendants and an insight into the making of the film.

It remains my favourite film ever since I first saw it in a London cinema in the summer of 1964. I was 11 years old at the time visiting the capital with my Mam and Dad, older sister Janet and younger brother Steve.

We were walking along the busy streets, looking in shop windows and marvelling at all the new sights. Suddenly Mam calls out, "Look Lulu's on, let's go and see her". Now I had heard of the wee lass from Scotland with the big voice, but I did not jump with excitement at the prospect of seeing her perform. Surely this great city can offer an 11 year old something a little more thrilling. But before I could say a word we turned left at a junction and the letter "L" was replaced by the letter "Z". Mam had only spied the last 3 letters and had presumed wrongly.

My face lit up as the word "Zulu" appeared in massive letters and my eyes were immediately drawn to the advertising photographs, showing in superb colour, scenes from the film.

Now it was Mam's face to drop as Dad summoned us all forward, and into the cinema trooped the Raby family. I was totally enrapt in the film for the whole 133 minutes and never wanted it to end. Indeed when the Zulus appeared near the end of the film to salute the brave men of the 24th regiment, I was hoping they would attack again. But all good things come to an end and I had the opportunity to watch it on another 2 occasions in my home town of York that same summer.

Now of course in the mid 60's there were no videos but this magnificent film seemed to come onto our screen every year over the Christmas holidays along with another great action film "The Alamo", which was one of John Wayne's masterpieces.

So the first thing I looked forward to at Christmas was getting my hands on the television magazine and flicking through it to see if it was on. If it was the family watched it, or at least the male members of our tribe did.

I have watched it uncountable times since on video and DVD and never lost my enthusiasm for it.

So read on, relive the moments and enjoy "Zulu - The Truth Behind The Film" by Paul Louis Raby.

MEET THE CAST

Stanley Baker, (Chard)

Born 28/2/28 in Farndale, Rhondda Valley, Wales. Died 28/6/76 in Malaga, Spain.

He was a big friend of Richard Burton, and they appeared on stage as juveniles in The Druid's Rest in Cardiff.

A dedicated socialist, he made political broadcasts for Harold Wilson's Labour Party in Wales and was active in the campaign for nuclear disarmament (CND). He was warned not to address a CND rally prior to the release of Zulu, in case his left-wing political activism hurt the film's performance in the United States.

Michael Caine, CBE. (Bromhead)

Born 14/3/33 in Rotherhithe, South London, he was the son of Ellen Frances Marie (nee Burchell), a cook and charlady, and Maurice Joseph Micklewhite, who was a fish market porter. His father was part gypsy and a catholic, but Caine was raised in his mother's protestant religion.

He grew up in Camberwell and during WWII was educated to North Runcton in Norfolk. Passing his eleven plus in 1944, he attended Hackney Downs Grocer's School. After a year he moved to Wilson's Grammar School, near Camberwell Green, which he left at 16 years old, after gaining six school certificates, which were abolished in 1951 following the introduction of GCE "O" level exams.

He worked briefly as a filing clerk and messenger for a film company in Victoria Street, and the Film Producer, Jay Lewis in Wardour Street. From April 1952-1954 he did National Service as a Fusilier in the Royal Fusiliers, serving at the BAOR HQ in Iserlohn, Germany and in combat in the Korean War.

When he first became an actor, he adopted the stage name Michael Scott. His agent informed him that someone else was using that name and he changed it to Caine, after seeing the film, "The Caine Mutiny" being advertised. He has since joked that had he looked the other way, he could have been called Michael "One Hundred And One Dalmatians".

In the early 1960's, he took a job as assistant stage manager for the Horsham based Westminster Repertory Company which led to walk on roles at the Carfax Theatre. After several minor roles he made the big time with "Zulu", followed by playing the spy Harry Palmer in "The Ipcress File," (1965) and the woman chasing title character in "Alfie", (1966).

He played Palmer another four times and made his first movie in the United States in "Gambit," (1966) opposite Shirley Maclaine.

In 1978 he starred in "Get Carter", a British gangster film, followed by "Educating Rita", (1983).

In complete contrast, he played Scrooge in "The Muppet Christmas Carol", (1992) and recently Alfred in Christopher Nolan's, Batman sequel, "The Dark Knight", (2008).

He has been Oscar nominated six times, winning his first Academy Award for the 1986 film, "Hannah And Her Sisters", and his second in 1999 for "The Cider House Rules", in both cases as a supporting actor.

Appointed Commander of the Order of the British Empire (CBE) in 1992 and in 2000 he was knighted as Sir Maurice Micklewhite, which was his legal name.

In 2008 he was awarded the prize for "Outstanding Contribution To Show Business", at The Variety Club Awards.

Married to actress Patricia Haines from 1955-1958, they had one daughter called Dominque. On 8/1/73, he married actress and model Shakira Baksh, and they too have a daughter, Natasha.

Chief Buthelezi, (Cetewayo)

Birth name, Ashpenaz Nathan Mangosuthu Gatsha Buthelezi, but he had a much shorter nickname, Gatsha.

A real life, distant relative of the Zulu king Cetewayo, he was a political leader, who founded the Inkatha, now the Inkatha Freedom Party. From 1970-1994, he was Chief Minister of Kwazulu Natal, the Zululand Territorial Authority in South Africa.

Subsequently, Home Affairs Minister under the multiracial government of Nelson Mandela and Thabo Mbeki.

After Zulu, he played another Zulu chief in Tokoloshe, (1971) and Chief Gatsha Buthelezi in "Zulu Dawn", (1979).

Jack Hawkins, (Witt)

Born 14/9/10 in Wood Green, London, he died on 18/7/73, three months after having an operation to have an artificial voice inserted.

His first film role was "The Four Just Men", (1921) and he made his theatrical debut in London at the age of twelve, playing the "Elf King" in "Where The Rainbow Ends".

Famous for his role as Captain Ericson in "The Cruel Sea", (1952) and Major Warden in "The Bridge Over The River Kwai", (1957).

In 1966, cancer of the larynx destroyed his voice, though he still acted, miming the dialogue that was dubbed post-production by either Charles Gray or Robert Rietty.

Ulla Jacobsson, (Margareta Witt)

Born in Gothenburg, Sweden, she is best remembered for playing the only female, speaking role in the film.

She was originally a stage actress and started appearing in English films in the early 1960's. Famously known for here nude scenes in "One Summer Of Happiness", where she took top prize at The Cannes Festival in 1951, she also starred in "Smiles Of A Summer Night", (1955).

Married to Swedish scientist Hans Winfried Rohsmann, her career tailed off in the 1970's and she died in Vienna from bone cancer at the age of fifty-four.

Patrick Magee, (Surgeon Reynolds)

Born 31/3/22, he died on 14/8/82.

Magee was a Northern Irish actor, best known for his collaborations with Samuel Beckett and Harold Pinter, as well as his appearances in horror films.

Born Patrick McGee in Armagh, Northern Ireland, he changed his name to Patrick Magee for the stage, after attending St. Patrick's Catholic College.

His first stage experience in Ireland was with Anew McMaster's Touring Company, performing the works of Shakespeare.

It was here that he first worked with Pinter, and in the same year as "Zulu", he joined The Royal Shakespeare Company. Pinter himself specifically requested him for the role of McCann, in his own play, "The Birthday Party".

Early film roles include, "The Criminal", (1960) and "The Servant", (1963). He went on to appear in "Young Winston", (1972) and "Chariots Of Fire", (1981).

He was married to Belle, a girl from his home town, and had twins, Mark and Caroline, who were born in London in February, 1961.

Known to be a heavy drinker, he died of a heart attack in 1982.

Dennis Folbigge, (Commissary Dalton)

Famously known for, "American Ninja 2 : The Confrontation", (1987) and "American Eagle", (1989).

He was one of South African radio's leading actor-writer-directors, and was responsible for adapting and directing many serials and series. Among these were, "The Avengers", upon which he worked for two years, having taken over the reins from Tony Jay, tailoring the original TV scripts for radio, and directing the recordings.

From time to time, he also worked in live theatre, his stage credits including plays such as "Amadeus" and "The Spider's Web".

Nigel Green, (Bourne)

Born on 15/10/24, in Pretoria, South Africa and died 15/5/72 in Dallington, East Sussex.

He studied at King's School, Wimbledon and then attended the University of London.

Following "Zulu", he played other military roles in "Khartoum", (1966), "Tobruk", (1967) and "Fraulein Doktor" and "Play Dirty", (both 1969).

Sadly, he died from an accidental overdose of sleeping tablets in 1972.

Paul Daneman, (Maxfield)

Born in London on 29/10/25, he attended The Haberdasher's Aske's School and Sir William Borlase's Grammar School in Marlow and studied stage design at Reading University, where he joined the dramatic society.

He followed "Zulu", with "Oh What A Lovely War", (1969), plus many TV appearances. He played the husband of Wendy Craig in the original series of the popular BBC sitcom, "Not In Front Of The Children", which began in 1967.

In 1995, he published "If I Only Had Wings", a novel inspired by his experience in the RAF during WWII.

He died on 28/4/01 and is buried at East Sheen Cemetery, South West London.

Joe Powell, (Windridge)

Born 21/3/22. Brother of fellow stunt performer, Eddie Powell, he was famous for his stunts from the 1940's to the 1980's, including "Zulu", and he played Anthony Quinn's stunt double in, "A High Wind In Jamaica", (1965).

In 2002, he spoke of his role in the film in "The Making Of Zulu, Roll Of Honour and He Snappeth The Spear In Sunder".

Gert Van Den Bergh, (Adendorff)

Born on 16/10/20, in Johannesburg, South Africa and died 16/2/68, in Cape Town, South Africa.

Gert acted in "Diamond Safari", (1958), and after "Zulu", "Seven Against The Sun", (1967) and "Rider In The Night," (1968), in the United States, before his early death that year.

Glynn Edwards, (Allen)

Born 2/2/31 in Malaya, he trained as an actor at Joan Littlewood's Theatre Workshop. He is best known for his role as Dave the barman and owner of The Winchester Club in the TV show "Minder".

He appeared in numerous TV shows, such as "Public Eye", "Some Mother's Do 'Ave Em" and "Dixon Of Dock Green".

He can be seen in rock band Marillion's video for "Heart Of Lothian" in 1985, where he plays a barman and Paul Young's video, "To Love Of The Common People" from 1983.

He also starred in a popular advert for McVities tea biscuits as "Jacko", famously quoting, "Yeah, I'll make a statement. A drink's too wet without one".

Married to actress Yootha Joyce from 1956-1968, he now spends his time between Spain and a house boat on the river Thames.

Dickie Owen, (Schiess)

Born in 1929, he was a taxi driver before "Zulu", in one episode of "The Saint," (1962), and a constable in "The Curse Of The Mummy's Tomb", (1964).

He followed this with some TV work, but like in real life, he seems a man of mystery, as a number of writer's for Britain's Film Review magazine have sought to track him down, without any success.

James Booth, (Hook)

Born David Geeves on 19/12/27 in Croydon, Surrey, England, he died on 11/8/05 in Hadleigh, Essex, England.

Son of a probation officer, he was educated at Southend Grammar School, which he left at 17 years old to join the army, and rose to the rank of captain.

He trained at RADA, then made his first professional appearance as a member of The Old Vic Company, before joining Joan Littlewood's Theatre Workshop at the Theatre Royal, Stratford East in 1958.

The Workshop's musical, "Fing's Ain't Wot They Used To Be", was a big hit and Booth looked set for stardom. Producer, Irving Allen saw the potential and signed him to an exclusive contract with Warwick Films.

Very busy in the 1960's, he will always be remembered for the part of Kenny Ames, a pornography baron, living in exile in Spain, in Series 2 of "Auf Wiedersehen", in 1985.

He did not become a super film star, due mainly to his alcoholism and his failure to work hard, which he openly admitted to. When not acting, he tried screenwriting and found a market in Hollywood.

From the mid 1970's – 1990's he lived in South Carolina, working as a scriptwriter with occasional film or TV appearances.

In late life he moved back to England, but never retired. He had two sons and two daughters to Paula Delaney, who he married in 1960, and his last film, "Keeping Mum", (2005) was dedicated to his memory.

Richard Davies, (593 Jones)

Born 25/1/26 in Dowlais, Merthyr Tydfil, Wales, he is best known for his performance as schoolmaster, Mr. Price, in the popular TV comedy, "Please Sir!"

He played Idris Hopkins in "Coronation Street" between 1974 and 1975, and also appeared in "Fawlty Towers", in 1979, as Mr. White, in the famous, "Kipper and the corpse" episode.

Another actor who appeared in "Dixon Of Dock Green", he also starred in "Softly Softly", (1966-9) and "The Sweeney", (1975).

Denys Graham, (716 Jones)

In his early days before "Zulu", he played flying officer L.G.Knight, D.S.O. in "The Dambusters", (1955) and Private Fraser in "Dunkirk", (1958).

A lot of TV work followed, including ten episodes of "Rumpole Of The Bailey", between 1983 and 1991.

Peter Gill, (612 Williams)

Born in Cardiff, Wales on 7/9/39, he was educated at St. Illtyd's College. He started work as an actor, both on stage, TV and on film.

His TV work included a royal navy radio operator in the TV series, "City Beneath The Sea", (1962).

He was the founder director of Riverside Studios in 1976, and became Associate Director of The National Theatre (1980-1997).

David Kernan, (Hitch)

Born in Eastham, London on 23/6/38, another actor who appeared in "Dixon Of Dock Green", before "Zulu", followed by nine episodes of "BBC3", (1966) and one episode of "Dr. Finlay's Casebook", (1967).

He played Nicholas in "Carry On Abroad", (1972) with Joan Sims and Kenneth Williams, who always ignored him. Also played Dr. Daly in the TV version of "The Sorcerer", (1982).

Gary Bond, (Cole)

Born in Liss, Hampshire, England on 7/2/40 and died in Ealing, England on 12/10/95.

In the same year as "Zulu", he performed in "The Indian Tales Of Rudyard Kipling", and an episode of "Z Cars".

He played another private called Staples in episodes of "Redcap" and "Misfire" in 1965, and did a lot of TV work in the 1970's and 1980's. In 1982 he acted in Sir Noel Coward's play, "Design For Living", performed at The Globe Theatre, London, with Maria Aitken and Ian Ogilvy, directed by Alan Strachan.

He also appeared in a series of "Bergerac" in 1990.

Ivor Emmanuel, (Owen)

Born in Margam, near Port Talbot, Wales on 7/11/27, he died on 20/7/07.

Ivor was a Welsh musical theatre and television actor, famous for leading the rendition of "Men Of Harlech" in the film's closing stages.

At 14 years old he was taken in by his aunt, when his family were killed by a stray bomb during WWII, and he began work in the coal mine. At the age of twenty, having failed an audition for the D'Oyly Carte Opera Company, he went for a drink with Richard Burton, who two weeks later, sent him a telegram, telling him to be at the Theatre Royal, Drury Lane the following day for an audition, and he was cast in the musical "Oklahoma!"

Other musicals followed, "South Pacific", (1951-1953) and "Damn Yankees", (1957). In May 1960, he performed in the first televised edition of The Royal Variety Performance, along with Benny Hill and Liberace.

He retired to Benalmadena on Spain's Costa Del Sol in 1984 and in 1991 he lost his life's savings of £220,000 in the collapse of the Bank of Credit and Commerce International.

He died in Spain in 2007 and was survived by his wife, Malinee and three children from his different marriages.

Neil McCarthy, (Thomas)

Born in Lincoln, England on 26/7/33, he died on 6/2/85.

Neil was a gifted linguist and pianist, who originally trained as a teacher.

He performed in "Clash of the Titans" and "Time Bandits" in 1981 and did a lot of TV work. This included "Dangerman", "The Avengers", "The Saint" and "Doctor Who".

He died of motor neurone disease, in Fordingbridge, Hampshire, England in 1985.

Larry Taylor, (Hughes)

Born 13/7/18 in Peterborough, England, and died on 6/8/03 in Johannesburg, South Africa.

Larry enjoyed a long and distinguished career, beginning in the 1940's, in "Dick Barton Strikes Again".

He did lots of film and TV work before "Zulu", followed by "Follow That Camel", (1967), "The Creeping Flesh", (1973), a grenadier in "Zulu Dawn", (1979), "Prisoner's Of The Lost Universe", (1983), and as Sheriff Hughes in "The Mangler", (1995).

He played Captain Birdseye in a series of TV commercials, and this swarthy, gap toothed character, was a familiar villain in British films and TV in the 1960's and 1970's, and because of his looks, he was often cast as an Arab or Mexican.

He was the father of stuntman, Rocky Taylor and died of a heart attack in 2003.

Kerry Jordan, (Cook)

A popular stage, TV and radio actor in South Africa, where he moved to in 1964, like many of his fellow British colleagues.

He had an early British film role in "The Flying Scot", (1957) and following "Zulu", played Reverend Bellow, in the very successful mini-series "Shaka Zulu", (1986).

His final TV credit before his death, was in "Where Angels Tread", a 1994 tele-movie about the early days of aviation, appearing alongside Diane Appleby and Clive Scott.

SCENE 1 – JANUARY 23, 1879

The film opens with a narration by Richard Burton as follows:

"The Secretary of State for War has today received the following dispatch from Lord Chelmsford, Commander in Chief of Her Majesty's forces in Natal colony, South Africa.

I regret to report a very disastrous engagement which took place on the morning of the 22nd January between the armies of the Zulu king, Cetewayo and our own number 3 column consisting of 5 companies of the first battalion, 24th regiment of foot and one company of the 2nd battalion, a total of nearly 1,500 men, officers and other ranks.

The Zulus in overwhelming numbers, launched a highly disciplined attack on the slopes of the mountain of Islandlwana and in spite of gallant resistance, the column was completely annihilated".

Up on the silver screen appears a picture of total devastation as hundreds of British redcoats lay dead, their bodies strewn all over the battlefield at Islandlwana, some slumped over the cannons they were defending, whilst wagons burn and smoke hovers in the air like death itself.

Enter the victorious Zulus, walking between the bodies, picking up the Martini-Henry rifles. A Zulu leader stoops and picks one up with a bloody bayonet attached and proudly displays it to the massed Zulu ranks up on the hill.

What follows is a film which Stanley Baker's wife, Lady Ellen, said, "Being a period film in costume it will never die". How very true.

SCENE 2 – CETEWAYO'S KRAAL

There is singing and dancing at the king's kraal, as according to the film trailer, 200 virgins are about to be married to 200 warriors, or "Old men", as Miss Witt describes them.

The Zulus were cattle herders and farmers who lived in village communities called kraals. They lived in cone-shaped houses which were made of straw and reeds. Zulu villages are shaped in a horseshoe or circle, with a fence perimeter and livestock pen in the middle.

Now we get our first glimpse of the Reverend Otto Witt, played by Jack Hawkins and his daughter, Margareta, played by Ulla Jacobsson, the only female with a speaking role in the entire film.

In real life, Swedish born Witt was a 30 year old married man with 3 small children. He had sent them away, with his long life wife, Elin, who was a teacher and a few years older than him, to the Gordon Memorial Mission House near Umsinga for their own safety.

Witt had purchased the 3000 acre farm known as Rorkes Drift in 1878 from James Rorke, an Irishman who had acquired it in 1849. The farm consisted of two buildings, Witt converting the store into a chapel and leaving the house for the family's living quarters.

Witt and Margareta are sat with king Cetawayo, played by chief Buthelezi, watching the wedding ceremony as a huge beast roasts over an open fire. Cetawayo beckons a young Zulu translator who then leans over to Witt.

Margareta: What did he ask father?
Witt: Whether a man of god like myself was pleased to see so many warriors married to so many maidens at one time.
Margareta: How can he imagine it would please anyone?

Witt:	Well do you think I said it pleased me daughter? I told him I was unhappy to see so many brides who may soon become widows.
Margareta:	That was a very good answer father.

The singing and dancing joyfully continues as Margareta looks on a little bewildered. The women sing holding miniature shields and the men respond moving forward with their weapons.

Margareta:	Why do they have those little spears? The girls I mean.
Witt:	It's a symbol of their chastity daughter.
Margareta:	Oh! (pause) It's splendid I know, but it's quite horrible too isn't it?
Witt:	The book says, "What went ye out into the wilderness to see, a man clothed in soft raiment?"
Margareta:	Yes father.
Witt:	You must understand these things if you're going to stay in Africa Margareta, that's why I brought you here. They are a great people.
Margareta:	But how can they let themselves be married in droves like this? Young girls to, to old men?
Witt:	In Europe, young women accept arranged marriages with rich men. Perhaps the Zulu girls are luckier, getting a brave man.

Suddenly a messenger stands at the entrance to the kraal and Cetawayo halts proceedings to wave the man forward. The messenger sprints forward and falls to his knees before his king. He tells him of the great Zulu victory at Islandlwana and the tribal chiefs gather quickly round their jubilant king.

Margareta springs to her feet and tries to run away, but is grabbed by her father who tells her to wait as he tries to find out what all the commotion is about.

Witt:	Oh lord in heaven.
Margareta:	What is it father?
Witt:	A thousand British soldiers have been massacred. While I stood here talking peace, a war has started.

The Zulus now begin to chant Ishiwan, Ishiwan.

Margareta:	Ishiwan? Didn't you say Ishiwan……
Witt:	Yes, it's their name for our mission station at Rorkes Drift. They are going to destroy it.
Margareta:	But why?
Witt:	Because there are British soldiers at Rorkes Drift.
Margareta:	There's only a handful.
Witt:	Come (and leads Margareta away).
Margareta:	It is a hospital, father tell him.
Witt:	Do you think he will listen? We must get there, there'll be a massacre.

As Witt and his daughter prepare to get on their two horse drawn buggy, we see the first Zulu casualty. This warrior was not shot by a Martini-Henry rifle or stabbed with a bayonet, but speared with an assegai by a fellow warrior on the king's order, for grabbing hold of Miss Witt.

As he slumps to the floor Witt drives hurriedly away to warn the garrison. Now look closely, because Witt has suddenly grown a dark beard.

Of course, Witt was not at Cetawayo's kraal. At this time he was probably observing the Zulu advance from the Oskarberg hill, which we will read about in Scene 3, and he never had a daughter of Margareta's age.

SCENE 3 – RORKES DRIFT

A rifle shot is heard, and we see Lieutenant John Rouse Merriott Chard, Royal Engineer's, played by Stanley Baker, who bore a striking resemblance to the real man, minus the moustache.

Chard was ordered by Lord Chelmsford to take men and equipment to Rorkes Drift, which he reached on 19/1/79. He took a light, mule wagon with Corporal Gamble, Sappers Cuthbert, Maclaren and Wheatley and his batman, Edward Robson. On arrival, he pitched his two tents on the Natal side of the river. Late in the evening of the 21st, Chard received an order to say that the men were to proceed to the column camp at Islandlwana. Having received no direct order himself, he got permission from his commanding officer, Major Spalding to go to the camp at Islandlwana, and see the orders.

The men travelled in the slow moving wagon, whilst Chard rode ahead. His orders were to keep the ponts at the river in working order and maintain the road between Helpmakaar and Rorkes Drift.

Lending a field glass, Chard could see a large force of Zulu's on the distant hills and decided to ride back to Rorkes Drift.

He met with Colonel Durnford and his mounted men and informed him of what he had just seen, and took orders and a message all along his line, at his request.

At the foot of the hill he met his men in the wagon, and making them get out, he took the wagon back with him. He of course did not know that he was leaving these poor men to their terrible fate.

Lieutenant Chard
Commanding Officer

Back at the camp Chard received the following order;

1. The force under Lt. Col. Durnford, R.E, having departed, a guard of 6 privates and one NCO will be furnished by the detachment 2/24th regiment on the ponts.

A guard of 50 armed natives will likewise be furnished by Capt. Stevenson's detachment at the same spot. The ponts will be invariably drawn over to the Natal side of the river at night. This duty will cease on the arrival of Capt. Rainforth's company, 1/24th regiment.

2. In accordance with Para. 19 regulations for Field Forces in South Africa, Capt. Rainforth's Company, 1/24th, will entrench itself on the spot assigned to it by column orders, Para. – dated -.

H. Spalding, Major Commanding

The above note was kept in Chard's pocket throughout the battle.

Back to the film and Chard is supervising work on the ponts with Corporal William Wilson Allen, another V.C. recipient, played by Glynn Edwards. Edward's said of himself, "It was my first proper film, although I had done a lot of theatre work", when interviewed later.

Allen was born in 1844, and attested in my home town of York, on 27/10/59, aged 15 years 8 months.

5 foot 4 inches tall he joined the regiment at Aldershot on 31/10/59. He served in Mauritius and South Africa and during his early service career was confined in cells, several times between 1860 and 1864. Re-engaged in 1873, he was posted to the Regimental depot on 21/4/74, where he was appointed Assistant Schoolmaster, receiving an extra 6d per day.

He was awarded a good shooting and judging distance prize in 1878, which no doubt served him well.

Helping with the work at the river, are some black natives, happily singing as they toil under the hot African sun, and several soldiers.

More shots are heard and Chard looks round. Meanwhile, back at the camp, cook checks his soup and Colour Sergeant Frank Bourne, played by Nigel Green keeps a wary eye on things. Now, Nigel Green looks Colour Sergeant material, tall, well built with a voice to match. However Bourne, who was 25 years old, was only 5 foot 5 inches tall and very thin. He volunteered at a Recruiting Centre in Brighton in December, 1872, aged 18 years old, and was posted to the 2nd battalion, 24th (2nd Warwickshire) Regiment in January, 1873.

He was promoted to corporal in April, 1875 and to his present position in April, 1878.

Well liked, he was affectionately known as "The Kid", by his men, whom some were old enough to be his father.

He commemorated the anniversary of the battle with a family dinner at home, and when asked about the battle said, "I consider myself lucky to have been there".

In the film, Bourne wears his stripes on his left arm, when they should have been on the right.

On a personal note, I have had the pleasure of visiting his grave at Beckenham Cemetery, Elmer's End Road, Kent. He died on 8/5/45, aged 90 years, just short of his 91st birthday and the end of WWII. Buried with him are his wife, Eliza Mary and Constance Ethel Bourne. He has a beautiful, white headstone and the final inscription reads, "Believed to be the last survivor of Rorkes Drift 1879".

This great man did a radio interview in December, 1936 called, "I was there", and replied to over 350 letters he received afterwards, which says a lot of him.

Now, back to the silver screen, the voice of Private Hughes, played by Larry Taylor booms out. There is no record of a Private Hughes.

Hughes (from a hospital window): Colour Sergeant Bourne, what's that shooting?
Bourne: A rifle Hughes.
Hughes: Eh!
Bourne: If your sick in hospital, I suggest you go and lie down.
Hughes: Yes Colour Sergeant.

Now, Hughes goes back into the hospital to ask his friend, Private Alfred Henry Hook, played by James Booth, who liked to be called Harry, what he thinks the shooting is all about.

Hook: Who do you think? Mr. flaming Bromhead, shooting flaming defenceless animals for the flaming officer's flaming dinner.

Hook is certainly correct as Bromhead has bagged a leopard, after missing it the first time, and a gazelle, being carried back to camp by native bearers, as he sits proudly on his horse.

The actor James Booth, was a big friend of Stanley Baker, who was godfather to two of his children, but his character in the film, is nothing like the real Hook. Private Hook, who won the V.C. for his gallant defence of the hospital, was a farm labourer before he enlisted as the result of a foreclosure on a mortgage in 1877, but most importantly, he was teetotal.

Such was the feeling of Hook's family at the actor's portrayal of him, Booth received many letters of complaint from them. He was actually in the hospital because he was a good cook, and his general duties were feeding the 30 odd patients, who were suffering with fever, lumbago, dysentery and trench foot.

In the film, the patients are idling the long hours away. They are bedded down in bunks, which were raised off the floor with bricks, with a bed of straw to lie on. Hook later described the hospital as, "A mere little shed, divided up into rooms so small, you could hardly swing a bayonet in them".

He was right of course, plus there were no interconnecting doors and some rooms which were windowless, opened directly outside.

When the Zulus attack the hospital building, we shall see what great problems this caused the defendants who were left to protect the patients.

Hook is passing time by trying to hustle another patient, with a game of "Find the bullet", hidden under one of three tin cups.

Sergeant Robert Maxfield, played by Paul Daneman, who is suffering from fever, interrupts the game singing, "Little Polly Perkin's of Paddington Green".

Maxfield attested at Newport on 30/7/75 aged 18 years 3 months, and was posted to 2/24th on 18/8/75. He was appointed Lance-Corporal on 25/5/76, Corporal on 11/11/76, and Sergeant in February, 1878.

Another good shot, he won a prize in 1878, but was too ill to be of any use during the battle.

In the film, Hook is annoyed with Maxfield's singing.

Hook: Shut up you cripple!

When Maxfield continues, Hook hits him with a belt, and carries on with his game.

Hook: Come on, make your mind up (to the patient I will refer to as the "player").
Player: (Looking at his bandaged wound). It's turning blue.
Hook: Yes, very pretty. Which one?
Player: It's under that one. (Pointing to the correct tin).
Hook: The boy's clever. The boy's good. How about putting some money on?

Maxfield interrupts again, this time shouting out orders.

Maxfield: Five rounds! Independent! Fire!

Hook:	Stuff me with green apples. You know, if a dog was as sick as him, they'd shoot him.
Maxfield:	Five rounds! Independent! fire!
Hook:	Shut up, you rotten sick ....

Totally frustrated, Hook shakes his sergeant vigorously.

Player:	Why don't you leave him alone? He's sick enough. You'll kill him.
Hughes:	Wouldn't bother Hookie, would it Hookie? Wouldn't bother Hookie at all, wouldn't matter at all if Maxfield was dead.
Hook:	(Sinking back on his bed, moans). Cor blimey! Rorkes Drift, take an Irishman to give his name to a rotten, stinking, middle of nowhere hole like this.

This is quite correct, James Rorke, born in 1821, was Irish and acquired the farm in 1849. He was a trader who dealt with both whites and blacks, the Zulus calling it Kwajimu, (Jim's Place). He was also a hunter who hunted the last of the elephants in the Mzinyathi Valley. He had a stock of guns, and did he sell some to the Zulus? I believe he was the sort of man who would if it meant him making money. Certainly the Zulus had plenty of smuggled firearms from other sources.

Rorke committed suicide in October, 1875, allegedly by shooting himself when he ran out of gin. He was buried under 3 foot of concrete in compliance with his last wishes, which I believe was to deter Zulu grave robbers, who had a custom of stealing European body parts, to use in their medicine.

The time is now about 2pm and two very important events take place, which the film ignores.

Firstly, Major Spalding, the commanding officer, confronted Chard and asked him whether he or Bromhead were senior. Chard did not know, so Spalding checked the army list. Returning, he comes out with a remarkable statement to Chard.

"I see you are senior, so you will be in charge, although, of course, nothing will happen and I shall be back again this evening, early".

Lieutenant Bromhead

Bromhead was made lieutenant in 1871, after been commissioned as an ensign in 1867, whilst Chard was made lieutenant in 1868, on graduating from Woolwich.

But the question must be asked, why did the commanding officer leave his post at such a perilous time, and give command to Chard, a man with no combat experience? His reason for leaving was to hurry up Rainforth's reinforcements which were overdue at Helpmekaar, but couldn't a rider on a fast horse do that?

Secondly, just after Spalding rode off, rifle and cannon fire could be heard in the distance, coming from Islandlwana. Three non-combatants, Witt, Rev. George Smith, who was the vicar of Estcourt, Natal and acting military chaplain, and surgeon James Henry Reynolds, on hearing this, decided that if they couldn't fight, they could at least look at what was happening.

The three men climbed the Oskarberg Hill, which Witt had re-named from Shiyane, to that of his Swedish king. On reaching the top, they discovered their view was obscured by Islandlwana mountain.

As they rested and listened to the gunfire, they spied a large number of natives which they took to be their own native contingent. But as they neared it proved to be two natives, (one presumably Prince Dabulamanzi, the king's half brother), mounted on white horses, heading a vast Zulu impi, and they wondered how such an army could have bypassed Chelmsford's column. With no time to lose, the trio raced down the hill to report what they had just witnessed.

As they descended, frantic riders fleeing Islandlwana cried out the unbelievable news that the camp was now in the hands of the Zulus.

Now back to the film again and Chard is still supervising the work, when one of the ponts floats free.

Chard: Hold that pont. Corporal Allen, get some men in the water.

Allen does this by pushing two laughing privates into the water, with the command, "You heard that officer of engineer's, get it!"

The two privates swim out and grab hold of the drifting pont, still laughing and joking with one another.

Meanwhile, Bromhead is approaching after his successful hunting trip. Partially deaf, Bromhead had served in The Cape Frontier War. He was a noted sportsman, being a champion boxer, wrestler and regimental cricketer and popular with his men, who nicknamed him "Gunny".

His commanding officer, Colonel Degacher had a lesser opinion of him, and described him as hopeless.

Bromhead (to Chard): Hot work?

Chard: Damned hot work.

Bromhead: Still the river cooled you off a bit, eh? Who are you?

Chard: John Chard, Royal Engineer's.

Bromhead: Bromhead, 24th. That's my post, up there. You've come down from the column?

Chard: That's right. They want a bridge across the river.

Bromhead: Who said you could use my men?

Chard: They were sitting around on their backsides doing nothing.

Bromhead: Rather you asked first old boy.

Chard: I was told their officer was out hunting.

Bromhead: Er, yes.

Bromhead digs his heels into his horse, moves forward then halts.

Bromhead: I'll tell my man to clean your kit.

Chard: Don't bother.

Bromhead: No bother, not offering to clean it myself. Still a chap ought to look smart in front of the men, don't you think? Well chin chin. Do carry on with your mud pies.

As Bromhead rides off, Chard hears a man singing.

Chard: What's your name?

Owen: Owen, sir.

There is no record of this name.

Chard: Are you supposed to be here?

Owen: Yes sir. Well not actually see sir, only you've got my solo tenor out there.

Chard: I've got your what?

Owen: 612 Williams sir. We were going to practice this afternoon with the company choir, but you've got my only solo tenor working out there in the cold water.

There were 4 Williams' present, but no 612.

They were, Private 1395 John, who won the V.C. He ran away to enlist and used his second Christian name of Fielding as an alias so he wouldn't be traced. Born in Abergavenny, Monmouthshire on 24/5/57 and attested at Monmouth on 22/5/77.

Private 934 John, born in Barristown and attested at Pontypool on 28/11/76. He died of disease at Rorkes Drift on 5/2/79.

Private 1398 Joseph, attested at Monmouth on 23/5/77, and was killed in the fight for the hospital.

Lance-Sergeant 1328 Thomas, who attested at Brecon on 6/3/77. He was mortally wounded in the battle.

Chard: Well I hope he sings better than he works.
Owen: Oh, indeed sir. He does.

Chard stamps on a piece of rotten wood used to secure the ponts.

Chard: Every piece of wood in this blistering country is eaten by ants.
Owen: Aye, the heat and the dust sir, very nasty on the larynx.
Chard: Mr. Bromhead let's you have a choir does he?
Owen: Well every Welsh regiment has a choir sir. Mr. Bromhead is English, but he is a proper gentleman.

Now here we have one of history's biggest myth's regarding the 24th regiment at Rorkes Drift. Owen has just said that it is a Welsh regiment, which is totally and utterly wrong. Some people even believe the garrison was manned fully by Welshmen. Well let me put the record straight, there wasn't enough Welshmen at Rorkes Drift to field a rugby union team at Cardiff Arms Park.

The mistake could have occurred because the 24th Regimental Depot was founded at Brecon, Wales in 1873, with most recruits joining the 2nd battalion. However, the 1st battalion had served abroad around the Mediterranean for the previous 8 years and had arrived in South Africa in February, 1875. The regiment carried the title, the 24th (2nd Warwickshire) Regiment Of Foot until 1/7/81, when county names were introduced under The Cardwell Act, and the 24th became The South Wales Borderers.

In 1881, Brecon only had a population of about 5,000 people and only half were males of all ages, therefore, the men of recruiting age for the army was very small.

Another fact is that during the Zulu war, mention of Wales as an entity was not officially recognised in any regimental documents or reports, and Lord Chelmsford always referred to the 24th as "English" in his reports.

One of the V.C. recipients, private Robert Jones, who was born at Penrose, Raglan, Monmouth, wrote,

"On the 22nd January, 1879, the Zulus attacked us, we being only a small band of English soldiers. My thought was only to fight as an English soldier ought to for his most gracious sovereign, Queen Victoria, and for the benefit of old England".

The best known figures of the number of defendants at Rorkes Drift are to be found in Norman Holme's, "The Silver Wreath" as follows.

49 English, 21 unknown, 18 Monmouthshire (then an English county), 16 Irish, 14 Welsh and 1 Scot, making a total of 119.

But, perhaps Stanley Baker who produced the film with Cy Endfield, and of course was a proud Welshman, wanted to glorify his homeland. After all the opening narration is by Welshman Richard Burton and there is a very strong Welsh theme throughout the film.

Even during the 14 weeks on location in Africa, Baker had Welshman Tom Jones' record, "It's not unusual," repeatedly played over loud speakers, to which the Zulu actors danced wildly to.

Also, the 24th regiment should have been recognised by the number 24 on their shoulders, but these are missing, perhaps an oversight.

So, back to the film, and Owen has just said that Mr. Bromhead is a "proper gentleman".

Chard: There's no doubt of that. And what do you sing?
Owen: Me, sir? Baritone sir.
Chard: Good. I can find work for baritones as well as tenors.

Chard then reaches for his binoculars, and after looking through them asks Owen.

Chard: See what you make of that, over there below the escarpment, two riders.

The riders were Lieutenant Adendorff of the Lonsdale Regiment, Natal Native Contingent, played by Gert Van Den Bergh and Lieutenant Vane, a carbineer who had met up on their escape from Islandlwana. They were the first to break the news of the massacre to Chard. The time is about 2.30pm.

Owen: Gallopers from the column sir?

Looking at the binoculars, he adds.

Owen: Very wonderful things these sir, aren't they?

Chard senses trouble, and don't forget he saw a large force of Zulus when he had earlier reported for orders at Islandlwana.

Chard (to corporal Allen): Get your party ashore at the double.

Quickly the party gathers at the river bank in formation.

Allen: Trouble sir?
Chard: Could be.
Allen: I can anchor the ponts midstream sir, with 6 riflemen I could ……….
Chard: This is a situation you think an engineer officer can't handle corporal?
Allen: No sir, beg your pardon sir.
Chard: Fall them in.
Allen: We ain't finished the bridge sir.
Chard: Fall them in corporal.
Allen: Sir.

The squad march back to the mission station. The time is about 3.15pm.
 Bromhead had already heard the news from a native despatch rider of the Edendale Contingent, who had been sent by Captain Edward Essex. After surviving the Zulu War, Essex had further lucky escapes during the Boer War, which earned him the nickname "Lucky Essex", and he went on to become instructor at Sandhurst, before commanding the Gordon Highlanders.
 Bromhead's reaction to the news was to bring the 2 wagons forward to prepare to evacuate the sick and he also ordered his men to bring out the mealie bags and biscuit boxes, so he was ready to move or stay and fight.
 Chard now goes over to Lieutenant Vane.

Chard: Ride like hell, tell them they can't get here too soon.

It was actually Bromhead who gave this order to Vane to ride to Helpmekaar for reinforcements.
 Back in the hospital a patient looking out calls, "They're building barricades or something!" to Corporal Christian Ferdinand Schiess, played

by Dickie Owen. 23 year old Schiess was born in Switzerland and was serving with the Natal Native Contingent. He was in the hospital suffering with a badly blistered foot, and as in the film needed a crutch to move about. Unfortunately no photograph exists of the man who liked to be called "Frederick".

There was a sad end to this brave fellow, when in 1884, ill and penniless he set sail back to England on board HMS Serapis. On the voyage home, he died and was buried at sea aged 28 years. The ship's log recorded his passing away on Sunday, 14 December, 1884 at 10.20 am. He was committed to the sea at 5.10 pm. Despite being penniless, his V.C. was removed from his body and brought back to England. After several years being locked away at the War Office, it is now on display at the National Army Museum in London.

Chard tells a corporal to get the native workers helping the cook, away from the camp.

Chard (to cook): Douse these cooking fires and turn the boilers over.

Cook: But they've got soup in them sir.

Chard: Pour it on the fires and get yourself a rifle.

Cook: A rifle sir? But I don't......

Acting Assistant Commissary, James Langley Dalton, played by Dennis Folbigge appears with the cook. Dalton served as a sergeant in the 85th Regiment (later the King's Shropshire Light Infantry) and he was discharged from the army in 1871 with the rank of Staff Sergeant. He is unfairly portrayed in the film as somewhat "whimpish", which he certainly was not.

Dalton: Mr. Chard, you've just asked this man to.........

Chard: To pour the soup on the fires. See that he does it, and all these bags of maize, inside the perimeter. And I don't want these tents providing cover for the enemy.

Chard kicks a guy rope away.

Chard highly respected Dalton and said of him after the battle, "His energy, intelligence and gallantry were of the greatest service to us".

Chard now had to make up his mind, whether to flee or make a stand on hearing the news from Islandlwana, but it was Dalton who suggested that they stay and fight. He pointed out that trying to flee with two wagons of sick patients over rough terrain, they would soon be caught by the running Zulus, and would stand no chance in the open. So it was decided to remain and make a stand and here Chard's engineering skill became invaluable as he organised the defence of the post using the mealie bags which weighed 200lb each and boxes weighing about 100 weight. The barricades went up quickly, as there were about 300 black troops of the NNC to help under the command of Captain William Stephenson, and there was a calm and confidence about the men who were sure Major Spalding would be returning soon with Rainforth's company.

Back in the film, cook complains to Dalton who advises him to speak to Bromhead, his own officer.

Chard introduces Adendorff, who brought Chard the news of the disaster, to Bromhead, who we know in reality had already heard about it from Captain Essex's despatch rider.

Bromhead: You've come from there? Alright man, is it true?

A light moment in the film now as cook approaches complaining about Chard's orders over the soup, which he had spent hours slaving over.

Chard: We have thatched roofs here Bromhead, no need to make the Zulus a present of fire.
Cook: Well am I to take a rifle too sir?

Bromhead ignores the cook as he turns to Adendorff.

Bromhead: The entire column? Well it's damned impossible, 800 men.
Adendorff: 1,200 men, there were 400 native levies also.
Bromhead: Damn the levies man, more cowardly blacks.
Adendorff: What the hell do you mean cowardly blacks? They died on your side didn't they? And who the hell do you think is coming to wipe out your little command, the Grenadier Guards?
Bromhead: What the deuce is the matter with him?
Chard: Adendorff, are you staying?
Adendorff: Is there anywhere else to go?
Chard: Talk to our levies will you? Tell them whose side their on.

Now, debate still continues regarding Adendorff's presence at the battle. He served with Lonsdale's Regiment, NNC, and was a lieutenant in Captain Krohn's No. 6 Company of the 1st battalion, 3rd NNC.

In the film he is present from delivering the news to Chard, right up until the end, but you don't see him in action. This man survived Islandlwana, so if he chose to go, like so many others, who can blame him?

He promised Chard he would stay and fight and with Corporal Francis Attwood, defended the storehouse, firing from loopholes. Featured in Chard's roll of honour, sceptics say he mistook Adendorff for Attwood, of the Army Service Corps, who received the Distinguished Conduct Medal for bravery at Pietermaritzburg in November, 1879.

It is rumoured that both Adendorff and Vane were arrested at Pietermaritzburg, but there is no evidence of a trial ever being held. So, the jury is out on this one and we will move on.

Chard: Did the runner bring orders?
Bromhead: He brought orders to the commander of this post.
Chard: To do what?
Bromhead: To hold our ground.

Bromhead did in fact receive a pencilled note from 4 colonial riders confirming the news and to hold his position at all costs.

Chard: To hold our ground? What military genius thought up that one, somebody's son and heir? Got a commission before he learnt to shave?

Bromhead: I rather fancy that he's nobody's son and heir now.

Chard spots the Witt's buggy approaching.

Chard: Who are they?
Bromhead: The Witt's.
Chard: Witt's?
Bromhead: The Swedish missionaries here. This is their station.
Chard: They've chosen a damned odd time for a prayer meeting.

Off course Witt was here, he'd just come down from observing the Zulu advance, but as I said before, his children had been sent away.

Chard: I think you'd better get them out of here.
Bromhead: You giving me an order, old boy?

Chard: Let's get one thing clear. I'm no line officer. I'm an engineer. I came here to build a bridge.

Bromhead: Jolly lucky for you eh? I mean otherwise you would've been chopped with the rest of the column.

Chard: Alright, what's the date of your commission?

Bromhead: Now don't tell me. I suppose you have seniority. 1872, May.

Chard: 1872, February.

Chard is clearly senior as I reported earlier by 3 years.

Bromhead: Oh well, I suppose there are such things as gifted amateurs, if I may………

Chard: Are you questioning my right to command?

Bromhead: Oh, not your right old boy. Never mind, we can co-operate, as they say. I'll be here won't I?

Chard: Bromhead, have you been here long enough to put a look out on that hill?

Bromhead: Erm, not since we've been chatting, no. Started the barricades though, managed to think of that.

This is true, and as Rorkes Drift was a supply depot and line of communication, there were piles of mealie bags and various boxes of meat and biscuits to build the barricades with. In charge of the stores were Assistant Commissary Walter Dunne, Acting Assistant Commissary James Dalton and Acting Storekeeper Louis Byrne.

Chard: Who's the sergeant with the muscles?

He is referring to Sergeant Windridge, played by Joe Powell, who is carrying two mealie bags comfortably.

Windridge was born in Birmingham, where he was attested on 26/1/59, aged 18 years 4 months. 5 feet 10 inches tall, which was above the average height, he served in Mauritius, East Indies, South Africa and Gibraltar. Promoted and demoted several times, he achieved the rank of sergeant on 27/4/77. Interviewed after, he said he had a more prominent role in the film, but had taken ill during shooting.

Bromhead: Sergeant Windridge, good man.

Surgeon James Henry Reynolds, played by Patrick Magee enters the hospital to treat Hook, who is complaining of a painful shoulder, and asks him to remove his vest so he can examine him.

Surgeon Reynolds was to be awarded the V.C. for his bravery in treating the wounded during the battle, but one thing about him in the film is missing. He had a fox terrier named "Dick", which stood by him throughout the battle.

Reynolds: You know what you've got there my malingering Hector?

Hook: No sir, er Hook's the name sir.

Reynolds: You've got a fine, handsome boil my friend. There's one glistening boil for every soldier in Africa. You may not win many medals on this campaign Hook but you'll certainly get more boils. For every gunshot wound I probe I expect to lance 3 boils.

He now produces a scalpel which terrifies Hook.

Hook: Er, er, a spot of medicinal brandy would set me up.

Let's not forget Hook was teetotal.

Reynolds: Brandy's for heroes Mr. Hook. The rest of you will make do with boils in your skin, flies in your meat and dysentery in your bellies. Now then, this is gonna hurt you a lot more than it will me I'm happy to say.

Reynolds is certainly enjoying his job at this moment, as he makes Hook whimper in agony.

Meanwhile, Witt has arrived and is dashing over to Bromhead.

Witt: Mr. Bromhead, Cetewayo is coming with 2 impis to destroy you.

The Zulus who actually attacked were the reserves who had not fought at Islandlwana, and who were hungry for action. It was the Zulu custom for the reserves to sit with their backs to the action so they would not get over excited and join in. Their job was to cut of the British forces retreat, but having missed out on the glory, Prince Dabulamanzi, whose name means "Part the waters", decided to attack Rorkes Drift, which was directly against the king's orders.

Dabulamanzi, was Cetewayo's half brother, and he had been ordered not to attack the British when they were encamped in a defensive position.

Brodhead (to Witt): You must talk to Lieutenant Chard, Mr. Witt. He commands here.

Bromhead salutes Margareta, being the gentleman he is.

Witt: Mr. Chard, I am ready to take away your sick and wounded. Please supply the wagons. Daughter tell the men in the hospital to get ready.

Chard: One moment Miss Margareta. Mr. Witt I don't suppose you hold the queen's commission?

Witt: I am a man of peace sir.

Chard: Then allow a queen's officer to give orders to her soldiers. Now, how do you know what Cetewayo is doing?

Witt: We have just come from his kraal sir. He's a member of my parish.

The Zulus were certainly not following Witt's preaching.

Chard: Your parish? Are you sure you're on the right side of the river, Mr. Witt?

Witt: I am here to do my duty. I expect your cooperation.

Chard (to Bromhead): What's our strength?

Bromhead: Er, 7 officers including surgeon, commissaries and so on, and oh, and Adendorff now I suppose, wounded and sick 36, fit for duty 97 and about 40 native levies. Not much of an army for you.

The figures are pretty close for the British, but there were a lot more native levies helping out at this moment.

Witt: There are 4,000 Zulus coming against you. You must abandon this mission.

Bromhead: Mr. Chard?

Chard: Adendorff sent his trooper to Helpmakeer. There's a relief column there, isn't there? Cavalry?

Bromhead: There was 3 days ago.

Chard:	Mr. Bromhead, issue all our walking wounded with arms and ammunition.
Witt:	You will all be killed like those this morning. And now the sick in their beds, all of you.
Chard:	I don't think so Mr. Witt, the army doesn't like more than one disaster in a day.
Bromhead:	Looks bad in the newspapers and upsets civilians at their breakfast.
Witt:	Sir, the good book says, "There is no king that can be saved by the multitude of a host, neither is any man………."
Chard (interrupting):	Mr. Witt, when I have the impertinence to climb into your pulpit and deliver a sermon, then you may tell me my duty.
Margareta:	It is not your duty to sacrifice the sick.
Chard:	Are you a student of tactics too, Miss Witt?
Margareta:	Are you a Christian?
Chard:	Sergeant Windridge.
Margareta:	It is your duty to let us take those men away.

As Margareta turns away, Chard calls out.

Chard:	Not that way Miss Witt.

Sergeant Windridge reports to Chard as Witt calls his daughter over.

Chard:	Sergeant, put two good men on that hill, tell them to keep their eyes peeled.
Windridge:	Mr. Bromhead, sir?
Chard:	Double up, dammit!
Bromhead:	Carry on sergeant, there's a good fellow.

In truth, Windridge was ordered to guard the casks of rum in the storehouse, with orders to shoot anyone trying to steal them.

Chard now calls for Colour Sergeant Bourne and Bromhead, and the three of them walk off together.

SCENE 4 – PREPARATIONS

The scene opens with a Welsh private called Thomas, Tommy in the film, holding a calf. Private Thomas was played by Neil McCarthy.

Thomas: You know, I had a calf once, back home in Merioneth. I'll get you some milk eh? I'll make you strong. Would you like that then?

Thomas is suddenly grabbed by sergeant Windridge.

Windridge: What the hell do you think you're doing at a time like this?

Thomas protests and is told to "shut up!"
    Meanwhile, as the barricades are being hurriedly built, private Owen starts to sing "Men of Harlech", and is joined by some of the other men, before he us called by Windridge.

Windridge: You've got a voice haven't you?
Owen: Yes, baritone, sergeant.
Windridge: Well get up on that hill and sing out if you see anything.

Windridge then orders Thomas to go with him, and they casually walk off together, with Windridge shouting.

Windridge: And take your bandook, you dozy Welshman!

As he yells, he throws Owen his rifle, which he had forgotten.

Adendorff now describes to Chard and Bromhead, the typical fighting tactics of the Zulus, which is true, and draws it in the ground with his bayonet.

Adendorff: The classical attack of the Zulus is in the shape of a fighting, bull buffalo like this. The head, the horns and the loins. First, the head moves forward and the enemy naturally moves in to meet it. But it's only a feint, the warriors in the head then disperse to form the encircling horns and the enemy is drawn in on the loins. Then, the horns close in on the back and sides.

He thrusts his bayonet into the sand and adds "finish", as Chard examines the drawing.

Bromhead: It looks er, jolly simple doesn't it?
Adendorff: Oh, it's jolly deadly old boy.
Bromhead (laughing): Well done Adendorff. We'll make an Englishman of you yet.
Adendorff: No thanks. I'm a Boer. The Zulus are the enemies of my blood. What are you doing here?
Bromhead: You don't object to our help I hope?
Adendorff: It all depends what you damned English want for it afterwards.
Chard: Alright (pointing). Hospital, church, cattle kraal, stores (drawing his plan in the sandy ground). An outside perimeter joining the buildings here and here. Now we don't move out to meet the feint of the buffalo head. We hold the outside perimeter. If and when that collapses we move back into this area here. How high can you build a wall, Bromhead?
Bromhead: Well, it should be about shoulder high. But if the fuzzies moved out of Islandlwana immediately, they could be here, well, now. It's just a matter of time.
Chard: Then we'll have to make the time.

Time is the one thing they haven't got, plus they didn't know the enemy strength, so the preparations needed to be done at the double.

Bromhead: You mean your only plan is to stand behind a few feet of mealie bags, and wait for the attack?

Chard: That's right. We wait.

Bromhead: If 1,200 men couldn't hold a defensive position this morning, what chance have we with 100?

Chard ignores the question and turns away.

Bromhead: I know exactly how to disperse them. Ambush, you see? We cut them down in the passes.

Bromhead never suggested this idea, his first two thoughts were stand or flee with the patients in the wagons.

Chard: Bromhead, I want that line of boxes across here, from the cattle kraal to the outside perimeter. If they get over this………redoubt, and a final redoubt here.

The redoubt was made from a huge pile of mealie bags, hollowed out at the top, in which he placed the wounded later on, and gave the men a high vantage point to fire from.

Certainly Chard's engineering skills were invaluable at this moment. He was determined to make the garrison as secure as possible in the short time he had before the Zulus came. Knowing that the Zulus main weapon was the close quarter, stabbing spear, which they thrust with using an upper arm movement, he was confident of holding them if he had the time to get the barricades high enough.

Both buildings were made of stone and had thatched roofs. The storehouse (church) was 80 feet x 20 feet and the hospital (house) was 60 feet x 18 feet, and they were about 30 yards apart.

The storehouse seemed secure as it had no doors or windows on the back wall, but the hospital was to prove a problem as I described earlier.

Chard suggested that the men make some type of communication through the hospital rooms, but it was not done, possibly because there was not enough time available. The men did knock loopholes through the outside walls, and blocked the doors and windows with mealie bags, boxes and mattresses.

The buildings stood on a flat shelf which dropped away a few feet in front of the them in a bank, 4 or 5 feet high. The front of the hospital was the weak spot, where only some planking closed a gap at one point and the barricade was not complete, due to it being the furthest point to carry the heavy mealie bags to. The mealie bags linked the two buildings and there was the added advantage of a 5 foot rocky ledge along the front, overlooking the orchard and the Witt's garden. When the mealie bags were placed on top of the ledge, the defendants had an 8 foot barrier to fight behind.

The two wagons were used in the back wall overlooking the cookhouse and ovens, and the water cart was already within the enclosure.

Although there would be plenty of cover for the Zulus behind trees and shrubs, there was a killing area all around the perimeter of about 40 yards. Chard's engineer's wagon was left by the rough kraal and his wagon driver freed the mules, which were rounded up safely the next morning.

The kaffir driver decided to leave and seek shelter in a cave. Finding a suitable spot, he settled down, but was alarmed when some Zulus entered armed with rifles and started shooting down onto the garrison. With return fire screaming back, the unfortunate man didn't know which side posed the biggest danger, but he survived to tell his tale.

It was at this point that Hitch, played by David Kernan, was sent to the top of the storehouse to act as lookout. Frederick Hitch, another V.C. winner, was a bricklayer's labourer who attested at Westminster Police Court on 7/3/77 aged 20 years 3 months. He had his V.C. stolen and a replacement was ordered by King Edward VII, which he received in 1908.

In the film, cook is looking totally bewildered by what is going on, as surgeon Reynolds enters the church with his medical staff, whilst the Witt's are busy collecting hymn books. Reynolds intends to use the church as his hospital.

In truth, when Witt came down from spying the Zulus advance, he saw a scene of destruction as the men were loop holing the walls and he saw his furniture scattered about his lovely home. Crying out "Mein Gott, mein wife and mein children", he rushed over to his horse and rode off with a sick, colonial officer. The Rev. Smith, who he had been with Witt, was about to do the same, but discovered that his groom had already fled with his horse, so he stayed and handed out the ammunition.

He was a rather eccentric, tall man, with a long, red beard and wore an alpaca frock which was frayed and going green with age.

Horrified Witt screams at Reynolds.

Witt: What are you doing in here? This is a church! Don't you realise, this is an altar table?

Reynolds: I'm sorry. There's nothing larger. We need it now. Damn it! There's no chloroform.

Witt (to Margareta): Go to the hospital. Tell the sick to be ready to leave.

Reynolds:	I want water, lots of it, a probe, a saw, some nitric acid. Don't take it too badly Mr. Witt. Isn't this as good a place as any for a man to be when he's in pain?

Witt has no answer, but to sneak out to the storehouse and take a stiff drink from a bottle he has hidden away, probably port or brandy. He then secretes it again and begins to pray.
    Enter Colour Sergeant Bourne with a couple of privates.

Bourne:	Excuse me sir (to Witt). Tuck your heads in afore they fall off (to the privates). Sorry, sir. I have orders to get some of these bags outside.
Witt:	I was praying that your officer may turn to god's word.
Bourne:	That's right sir. A prayer's as good as a bayonet on a day like this.
Witt:	Have you prayed?
Bourne:	There'll be a time for it, sir.
Witt:	What will you say?
Bourne:	Bit of the psalms, I suppose sir. My father was a lay preacher. A great one for the psalms, he was. There was one, well might have been written for a soldier.

Bourne was actually the youngest of 8 sons, and his father was a farmer.

Witt:	Say it, man. Lift your voice to god.
Bourne:	Now sir?
Witt:	Yes. Let them hear your voice.
Bourne:	They know my voice when they hear it sir.
Witt:	Let them hear it know in praise of the lord. Call upon him. Call upon him man, for your salvation.
Bourne:	Well, as far as I can remember sir, it goes something like this. "He maketh wars to cease in all the world, he breaketh the bow and snappeth the spear in sunder". Do you know it, sir?
Witt:	"I shall be exalted among the heathen, I shall be exalted in the earth. The lord of hosts is with us".
Bourne:	That's it sir. (Turning to the 2 privates). Alright, nobody told you to stop working. You lead back-sided………Get sweating.

Over in the hospital, Margareta is tending to sergeant Maxfield.

Hook: I've been sitting there thinking. I've got it all sorted out. (He spots Margareta). Wey, company.
What are you doing here, miss? He doesn't need any help, I'll look after him, won't I?

Laughing loudly, Hook climbs on to his bunk.

Margareta: You are all to be evacuated soon in the wagons.
Hook: Who says?
Margareta: My father.
Hook: Oh, that's nice isn't it? Your father, eh?
Private: You and me Hookie, Mr. Chard's orders, in this room.

The private hands Hook a rifle.

Hook: What are you talking about? I'm sick. I'm excused duty.

A private begins to make a loophole in one of the walls, using his bayonet.

Margareta: What are you doing?
Private: I'm making a loophole, see? Me and Hookie's gonna fight in here, aren't we Hookie?
Hook: You're joking, I'm sick. Nobody's got any right to ask me to muck around in a flaming battle. I'm getting out.
Maxfield: Private Hook.
Hook: Yes.
Maxfield: Yes, sergeant. I know you Hook.
Hook: Yeah, you ought to.
Maxfield: You're no good Hook.

Maxfield pulls himself up with the aid of a rifle.

Maxfield: They gave us you because your no good to anyone except the queen and sergeant Maxfield.
Hook: Thank you very much, the both of you.
Maxfield: Take this rifle, Hook, and get to it! I'll make a soldier of you yet.

Hook:	And what for? Did I ever see a Zulu walk down the city road? No! So what am I doing here?
Maxfield:	You are here because you were a thief and you still are one.

No doubt this will have upset Hook's family, resulting in the letter's, and more slanderous remarks are mentioned by Bromhead to Chard later on.

Hook:	Certainly.
Maxfield:	Hook, my lad, and now you can be a soldier, like what they pay you for.
Hook:	Look, you got me 28 day's field punishment in Brecon. Isn't that enough?

Hook never received this punishment, and I very much doubt he had ever been to Brecon. The regiment was serving abroad before the South Africa campaign.

Maxfield:	Pick up the bayonet and help Williams.

Hook reluctantly makes an attempt to make a loophole, with the bayonet.

Maxfield:	And put your tunic on!

Getting annoyed, Hook turns around and glares as Maxfield collapses to the floor. Bayonet in hand, Hook walks over as Margareta looks nervously on, and picks Maxfield up on his shoulder.

Hook:	28 day's field punishment. No pay. Know what he did? Sent money to my missus. (He slaps Maxfield on his backside). What did you do that for?
Margareta:	You hate him for it?
Hook:	What do you want me to do? Cry my heart out? Give him a big kiss?
Margareta:	I thought you might pray for him. (Margareta leaves the room).
Hook:	Oh, she's a dry one. Very cool. You know what she needs?

Margareta hears this as she stands outside the door, then walks away as inside the men joke about her, and enters another small room.

Margareta: Can I help anyone? There will be wagons soon to take you away.

She looks at a sick man who reaches out to her.

Scheiss: He's dying. There's nothing you can do.
Margareta: Nothing? There must be.

Chard now enters with sergeant Windridge.

Chard: Are there any walking sick without rifles?
Scheiss: Me.
Windridge: You Dutchy? You couldn't walk to the latrine.
Scheiss: This is not my first action. Come on.
Margareta: Are you expecting sick men to fight?

Chard and Windridge leave the room.

Private 716: What's he going to do, 593?
Private 593: Oh! I think he wants to be a hero 716.
Schiess: Haven't you rednecks got names instead of numbers?
Private 593: This is a Welsh regiment, man. Though there are some foreigners from England in it.

593 was played by Richard Davies and 716 by Denys Graham.
    Again we cannot escape the Welsh references, and the funny thing is, there were 2 private Jones, numbers 593 and 716, and both were born in England. Good on the foreigners.

Private 593: I am Jones from Bwlchgwyn (should be Evesham in Worcester). He is Jones from Builth Wells (should be Penrose, Raglan, Monmouth). There are 4 more Jones' in "C" company. Confusing, isn't it Dutchy?

There were only 5 not 6 Jones' at Rorkes Drift. The above 2 plus privates John 970, John 1179 and Evan 1428, and they were not in "C" company, it was "B" company.
    There would be 6 Jones' if 593 was counting singer Tom Jones, mentioned earlier.

Private 593:	What's your name then?
Scheiss:	It's Scheiss. And I'm not Dutch, I'm Swiss.
Private 716:	Well there's a silly man, by damn. He's got himself into a private war.
Scheiss:	I belong to Natal Mounted Police.
Private 593:	Is that true then? He's a peeler 716. Come to arrest the Zulus.
Scheiss:	What do know about Zulus?
Private 716:	Bunch of savages, isn't it?
Scheiss:	Hmm! Alright, how far can you rednecks march in a day?
Private 716:	Oh, 15, 20 miles is it?
Scheiss:	Well a Zulu regiment can run, run 50 miles and fight a battle at the end of it.

The Zulus crossed 15 miles over rugged terrain at the run to reach Rorkes Drift, and with their long, loping stride over such ground, were faster than a horse.

Private 593:	Well, there's daft it is then. I don't see no sense in running to fight a battle.
Scheiss (to Margareta):	What are you doing here at such a time like this, why don't you go?
Margareta:	No. Not until you have gone.
Scheiss:	You know Cetewayo has a regiment of young girls, warriors, called, "Ripen at noon".
Private 593:	There's pretty.

As Margareta continues to nurse the sick, a patient grabs her, ripping her dress, as he tries to steal a kiss from her. As the men laugh, she flees from the room with their laughter ringing in her ears.

Private 593 (On coming out of the hospital):	Hey! Hey! Boys! Take a look at this.
Private (From Window):	What is it boyo?
Hook:	Flaming dust. What else?
Private:	No by damn, it's horses.
Bandaged patient:	It's the cavalry.

Hook: It's the relief column, you long range sniper, you.

Chard calls Colour Sergeant Bourne and Bromhead, and looks pleased as the rider's halt. The leader introduces himself as Stephenson, Darnford's Horse.

Captain William Stephenson, a colonial of the NNC, who commanded 200-300 natives, was already helping with the defences as stated in scene 3. He and his men did not stay to fight like the film's Stephenson's.

In the film, Stephenson's men are white, who I take to believe are colonials, possibly Boers, riding home to protect their farms. I think Stephenson here should have been portrayed by Lieutenant Henderson of the Mounted Natal Native Horse, who offers to help at first. He had arrived at 3.45pm with about 100 men and deployed behind Shiyane Hill, to stall the Zulu advance. Unfortunately, on engaging the first Zulu skirmishers about 45 minutes later, they fled.

No action was taken against Henderson, and Chard did not blame them. He even spoke well of them when he saw them fighting later on in the war.

Chard: Thank god you're here.
Stephenson: I'm surprised you're still here. Do you know there are 4,000 Zulus coming this way?
Chard: We know. Can you throw out your men in a screen to the south of here? You know how the Zulus feel about cavalry.

This is what Chard actually asked Henderson of The Mounted NNH to do, which he did at first.

Stephenson: I know what my men feel about Zulus. We've only just got through them.
Bromhead: Stephenson.
Stephenson: Bromhead. What price this? You know your whole regiments gone?
Chard: Bromhead. You know this man? Tell him we need him.
Stephenson: I'm sorry. I'm sorry. Look at my men.

Stephenson wheels his horse around to leave.

Chard: Stand fast, stand fast, all of you. Where the hell are they going? Get them back here, (grabbing Stephenson's bridle).
Stephenson: Let go of my bridle!

Chard: Get them back here.

Stephenson: If they're going to die, they'll die on their own farms. You're the professionals. You fight here if you want to.

Stephenson rides away, following his men as Chard calls after him.

Chard: We need you! Don't go! Don't go! Stay! We need you, damn you. We need you.(Turning to Bromhead). You didn't say a single word to help, Bromhead.

Bromhead: Oh, when you take command, old boy, you're on your own. The first lesson, the general, my grandfather, ever taught me.

Work on the barricades stops as the men watch in disbelief as the riders disappear in the dust and an eerie silence hangs in he air. It is suddenly broken by a loud, booming voice.

Bourne: Alright, then. Nobody told you to stop working.

The native levies under Captain Stephenson are agitated by the desertion, and speak in their native tongue to one another, as Witt approaches.

Witt: Brothers! O Brothers! The way of the lord has been shown to us. Thou shalt not kill, saith the lord. Brothers! O brothers! God's love is peace.

Chard calls for Bourne.

Witt: Go in peace. Stay not to kill and be killed. Go I say.

Some of the natives take his advice and skip away.

Witt: The sin of Cain will be upon you. "Am I my brother's keeper?" asked Cain. "Yea, we are all our brother's keeper".

With that, the remaining natives flee.

Witt: The nations are but a drop of the bucket, and are counted as the small dust of the balance.

Two privates now come over and grab the spouting Witt.

Bourne: Bring him along.

Chard: Mr. Witt, I'm getting you off this post.

Windridge: Sir, they've all hopped it. All of them.

The natives under Stephenson, actually left the camp when they saw Henderson's horsemen move out, which was at about 4.30pm. When Stephenson and his 2 white NCO'S also followed, shots were fired at them by some of the defendants in anger, and a corporal Anderson was killed. No order to open fire was given and the matter was overlooked, although Anderson's name is listed as "Killed in action", in official records.

The garrison had now been greatly reduced to just over 100 men, and Chard immediately organised the construction of a wall of biscuit boxes across the centre of the compound, to fall back on. A tactically sound idea, it however isolated the hospital, as Chard tried to man the whole of the perimeter.

He then sent out Bourne with a small body of skirmishers to try and hold up the enemy advance. Bourne wrote, "I was instructed to take out and command a line of skirmishers, and about 4.30pm the enemy came in sight round the hill to our south and driving in my thin red line of skirmishers, made a rush at our south wall".

All along fugitives had been passing by, only stopping to warn the garrison, who ceased work and huddled round to hear the terrible news. They said they must all leave as staying would mean certain death.

Passing fugitives included a Natal Carbineer, called Fletcher, privates Grant and Johnson of the 1st Battalion, who had been with the Rocket Battery and 2 mounted policemen, named Shannon and Doig, who all had the same story to tell. Hearing these tales must have been a confidence shattering blow to the defenders, but to a man they did not falter and stayed at their posts. Now back to the film.

Witt: Give me those wagons and I will save the sick.

Chard: You want the wagons? Mr. Bourne. Windridge. Get those wagons in.

Witt: God loves a sinner come to his understanding.

Hook (Out of hospital window): Hey, we're in luck. Hey, looks like the old parson got Chard to let us go.

Witt is looking very pleased with himself as the wagons are trundled forward, but is horrified when Chard motions to have them upturned and included into the defences. One wagon is tipped over and crashes to the ground, followed by three more, as Witt tries hopelessly to try and correct one of them.

There were in fact only two wagons used in the fortifications, which were situated in the south wall, overlooking the Oskarberg, (Shiyane) hill and the rocky terrace, from which the Zulus would soon be firing down onto the post from.

These two wagons were not overturned, and had mealie bags and boxes filling in the gaps underneath, with some on top for extra height.

Witt: O lord god, give me strength. Oh, god! God forgive me. I have the strength of thousands while the spirit of god is with me.

Chard: Colour Sergeant Bourne.

Witt: Oh, god forgive me.

Chard: Get him away from here.

As Witt is led away, Margareta dashes over.

Margareta: Leave him alone! Leave him alone!

Chard: Miss Witt!

Margareta (slapping Chard's face):   Animals! All of you! Animals!

Chard: Sergeant Windridge.

Witt: We shall not go. If you send us away, we shall come back.

Chard: Lock him up. Lock him in the storeroom. Put a man on the door.

Now, is this a good idea from Chard? Remember the casks of rum are in there, and our Mr. Witt is partial to a tipple.

Chard: Alright you men. Get back to work. And you..........! (looking at Miss Witt). Put Miss Witt in the church with surgeon Reynolds.

Sergeant Windridge picks Miss Witt up under one arm and carries her away, as she cries out.

SCENE 5 – LIKE A TRAIN IN THE DISTANCE

Privates Owen and Thomas are on look out duty high on a hill.

Thomas: It was sad you know, and sick. Had a battle coming, see? Animals are very sensitive to noise, you know.

Owen: Why worry about a calf?

Thomas: I thought I was tired of farming. No adventure in it. But when you look at it, this country's not a bit as good as Bala and the lake there. Not, not really green like. And the soil, there's no moisture in it. Nothing to hold a man in his grave.

Thomas bends down and clutches a handful of dry grass, whilst in the distance, a thumping noise can be heard. Meanwhile, back at camp, Chard and Bromhead are in conversation.

Bromhead: Chard. One of my men, Hook. Do you know him?

Chard: No.

Bromhead: In the hospital, malingering, under arrest. He's a thief, a coward and an insubordinate barrack room lawyer, and you've given him a rifle.

Chard: What?

Bromhead: In Queen's regulations, it specifically states….

Chard raises his arm to stop Bromhead as they both listen to the noise in the background.

Bromhead: Damn funny, like a, like a train in the distance.

Looking out, they can't see anything and the whole garrison stops work to listen to the rhythmic thumping noise, which is the advancing Zulus, banging their spears against their shields.

Chard: You were saying about Hook?

Bromhead doesn't answer as Colour Sergeant Bourne approaches.

Bourne: Mr. Bromhead, Sir. Sentries have come in from the hill. They say….
Chard: Colour Sergeant. You have something to report?
Bourne: Sir.
Chard: Then tell me.

Bourne looks across to Bromhead, who nods to him.

Bourne: Very good. Sir. The sentries report Zulus to the southwest. Thousands of them.
Chard: Alright, Colour Sergeant, stand to.

Bourne in fact, would have been one of the first to see the Zulus, because earlier he had been sent out with a line of skirmishers to try and slow down the Zulu advance.

Bourne: Stand….to.

The bugler calls the men to arms, who rush and grab their rifles and take their positions at the barricades. In the background, the cook and Dalton are opening boxes of ammunition.

Bourne: Look to your front. Mark the orders. Mark the target when it comes. Look to your front.

Repeating the order Bourne walks along the defences, as corporal Allen is giving the same order.

Bourne: Hitch, do your tunic up.
Hitch: My tunic?
Bourne: Do it up. Where do you think you are, man?

Hitch was actually brewing tea, then he was stationed as look out on the roof of the storehouse. He does his tunic up, and I must say the men look immaculate, in their single breasted red tunics with green facings, dark blue trouser with red stripe and low brimmed, white tropical helmets. The men in "B" company had learned the veteran's trick of dulling their helmets and pouches with tea and coffee, which we don't see in the film. The men look as if they are on the parade ground, but this is for the big screen only. After months of campaigning their uniforms would have been very ragged, certainly dusty and probably patched up, and their boots would not be gleaming, but worn and split after miles of marching across rough terrain. The order to, "Look to your front and mark your target", is repeated by Bourne and Allen. Meanwhile, the private guarding Witt at the storehouse is looking very nervous.

Witt: Boy, hear me boy. Will you be Cain and kill your brother? "Thou shalt not kill", saith the lord. You believe in the lord's word, don't you? Obey the word, boy. Obey the lord. Go to the others boy, go to the others.

Just as the very edgy private seems to falter, Colour Sergeant Bourne comes up to him.

Private: He's …. Mr.Witt says…..

Bourne: Never mind him, boy. Now you get along back to the ramparts with your mates.

Private: Yes Sir.

Bourne: Mr Witt, Sir. Be quiet now, will you? There's a good gentleman, you'll upset the lads.

Chard paces nervously as he and Bromhead await the Zulu attack.

Bromhead: You know my father was at Waterloo?

Yes, Bromhead was born at Versailles in France. He was the third son of Edmund De Gonville Bromhead, a baronet and lieutenant, who fought at Waterloo.

Chard: He was?
Bromhead: He got his colonelcy after that.
Chard: Did he?

Bromhead:	And my great-grandfather, he was the Johnny who knelt beside Wolfe at Quebec.
Chard:	Did they make him a colonel too?
Bromhead:	No, you don't see what I'm driving at.
Chard:	You're telling me that you're the professional, I'm the amateur.
Bromhead:	No. What I mean is, I mean, I wish right now I were a damned ranker, like Hook or Hitch.

He selects two V.C. Winners here

Chard:	You're not, are you? You're an officer and a gentleman.

The rhythmic thumping noise is getting louder.

Bromhead:	Listen. That damn train again.

The garrison is standing at the ready. Back in the store house, Witt smashes a window and yells out.

Witt:	"He breaketh the bow and snappeth the spear in sunder!"
Bourne:	"I will be exalted among the heathen, I will be exalted in the earth. The lord of hosts is with us."
Allen:	I hope so. As I live and die, I hope so.

The rhythmic thumping suddenly stops, and everything is quiet.

SCENE 6 – FIX BAYONETS

Chard looks out through his binoculars and nods to Bromhead.

Bromhead: Company will fix bayonets! Fix! Bayonets! Atten-shun!

Hitch drops his bayonet which clangs on the ground and corporal Allen calls him a "slovenly soldier", but as stated in scene 5, Hitch was looking out from the storehouse roof.
    The bayonet itself could be as long as 24inches, and with its long reach was nicknamed "the lunger". It was capable of pinning a man to the ground, but during the battle a lot were snapped or bent. Now we see our first shot of the attacking Zulus, and what a magnificent view, backed up by a brilliant soundtrack, which adds to the tension. The camera spans across from left to right, and we see thousands of Zulus on top of a hill in a line, with the main body lower down on the right. The first real sighting was observed by Private Hitch on the storehouse roof when asked "how many?" by Bromhead, he replied "4 – 6 thousand". Then a voice with a strange sense of humour called out, "Is that all? We can manage that lot very well for a few seconds".
    In an interview actor Glynn Edwards, who played corporal Allan said that there were only 500 Zulu actors employed in the shooting of the film. Therefore, the appearance of the mass ranks of the Zulus had to be carefully staged. What the film crew did, was to nail 10 shields to a baton of wood with plumes on the top, and a Zulu actor at each end. Thus, making every 2 Zulus look like 12. He added that if you look very closely, 10 of them have no legs.
    Whilst I am on the subject, the filming was delayed on location by freak weather, and it actually snowed ice balls. The cameras did not roll for the first 7 days and the Zulu actors brought in a real witch doctor to try

and change things. He turned up with his magical bones in a bag and one through his nose. He then marked out some chalk signs, which the cast never touched throughout the entire filming for fear of bringing on bad luck. He did a dance, but all to no avail and the bad weather continued for a further 5 days.

During this time some of the battle scenes were rehearsed indoors. Now, all the spears and bayonets used in the film are real and fortunately there were no serious injuries, only some scratches and bruises.

The amazing thing with the Zulu actors, is that they had never seen a movie before and all the equipment that makes one. Stanley Baker had a brainwave, and having a huge rock painted white, gathered them round and proceeded to show them old black and white films of Harold Lloyd, Buster Keaton and Laurel and Hardy, which absolutely fascinated them. We shall see later on when the battle begins and they are getting shot, they do a lot of "overacting", which I believe is the result of watching these old films. It is now day 13 on the set, and Mrs. Baker rose at 4.30am to be greeted by a clear blue sky and rushed round to wake everyone up. After she made tea, filming began. So back to our film.

Chard and Bromhead look on as Bromhead swallows hard and they check their revolvers.

On another personal note I visited The Royal Engineer's Museum in Chatham, Kent, especially to see the Zulu war display. There are some splendid pieces on show in the Zulu war gallery, including a white, marble bust, depicting Chard, wearing his patrol jacket, with one star each side of the collar. It is 2 foot 6 inches x 1 foot 8 inches wide on a black plinth, which is 3 foot 10 inches high, 1 foot 6 inches square, tapering to 12 inches at the top. There is also Chard's sword from the battle, it is a royal engineers' pattern sword, with gold sword knot, serial number 15869, marked JRMC and "Nil Desperandum". It has a steel scabbard, brass top marked, "Wilkinson, Pall Mall" and is fitted with a leather holder. The sword itself, measures 985mm long. Chard's cloth covered oval water bottle with leather strap is also there, but the most precious piece for me, was the revolver used by Chard at Rorkes Drift. It is a Webley .45 revolver, Ric model no.1450C.F. service no.40916 and the top of the barrel is marked, "Army and Navy C.S.L.".

On the Zulu side, there are shields in white skin with a wooden centre support, and wooden knobkerries, which are wooden clubs with spherical heads, a weapon used by the Zulus but not used in the film. Unfortunately Chard's revolver was not on display. On asking its whereabouts, I was told that it was locked away in the armouries for safe keeping as a lot of building work was going on in the museum. Disappointed, I accepted the situation and carried on my tour. As I was about to leave, I was called by one of the staff and told that someone was coming to see me. Waiting a couple of minutes, I was greeted by two other members of staff, one who carried a huge set of keys, and led to the armouries for a personal viewing. Being handed a pair of white gloves which the snooker referees have, I was allowed to hold Chard's revolver, plus a Martini-Henry rifle and had photographs taken, which was a fantastic bonus, when I was only expecting to view these items in a glass cabinet. The revolver I found was very light, and holding it I wondered how many Zulus had died from its bullets. The revolver in the film is much older than would have been around in 1879, and I believe it is a World War 1 issue revolver. Thanking the staff, I signed the visitors book, and you can read my comment to them, dated 23rd January 2008, and I take this opportunity to thank Beverley Williams, Assistant Curator and the staff once again.

I toasted my luck in the nearby local, aptly named, "The Engineers Mate", with a pint of lager. Sitting down to enjoy it I spotted a painting from Rorkes Drift with Chard prominent and walked over for a closer look. I'd seen the picture before, but at the bottom this one described Chard as being with the South Wales Borderers. I wasn't going to let this howling mistake spoil my day, so I ordered another pint.

Back in the film, Chard checks his binoculars again, as all around there is an eerie, deadly silence.

What must have been going through these men's minds? They knew the Zulus took no prisoners, so it would be a fight to the death. Rumours of friends agreeing to shoot each other if need be are equalled by men saying they will fight on and kill as many of the enemy as they possibly can. Nerves of steel are needed and we shall see that these brave men were made of the finest.

SCENE 7 – LOAD, PRESENT, FIRE!

Bromhead: Load!

The soldiers were using the Martini-Henry rifle, which was brought into service in 1871. It was a single shot, breech loading rifle, weighing just over 9lbs, capable of firing 12 rounds per minute. It had a range of over 1000 yards, but was most effective at 400 – 450 yards.

The major problem with the rifle was that after a lot of use, which was certainly the case at Rorkes Drift, the barrel became hot, making it hard to handle and the bullets would jam, requiring a ram rod to free it. This obviously slowed down the weapon's effectiveness, plus the recoil forced the men to keep switching shoulders as they became sore and bruised.

The Zulus in the film beat their spears against their shields as their leaders signal and the Zulus begin chanting.

Bromhead: North rampart, stand fast! South rampart, at 100 yards! Volley fire! Present!

The Zulus did attack the South wall first, with a body of about 600 warriors of the Indluyengwe regiment who were unmarried men in their early thirties, but the Martini-Henry rifle should have been put to good use well before the order to fire at 100 yards.

On the arrival of the Zulus, a voice shouted out, "Here they come! As black as hell and as thick as grass". I always believed it was private Hitch from his lookout position on the storehouse roof, who shouted this out, which is verified in Michael Glover's "Rorkes Drift". However, in "The washing of the spears", Donald Morris claims it is Private John Wall whilst Saul David in his book "Zulu" says it is Sergeant Henry Gallagher, who was in charge of the South wall. As an ex-bookmaker, I will go for the reverse forecast of Hitch and Gallagher.

The Zulus charged forward towards the South wall, dressed in loin cloths with horse hair fringes and animal tails streaming from their elbows and knees. Many wore cow tail necklaces and bead work ornaments. Some wore a single chrome feather on an otter skin head band, and horned snuffed boxes hung from their necks and earlobes. They have the usual spears, the short assegai used for stabbing in hand to hand confrontation and several longer ones for throwing at distance. However, there is no sign of the knobkerry, a wooden club with a spherical head, capable of smashing a man's skull. If you have seen the film "Zulu Dawn", you will have noticed this hand held weapon being used most effectively.

On my visit to The Royal Engineer's museum at Chatham, there were Zulu war axes on display, which I have not noticed in either film.

In the film, the order to fire and reload is given by Bromhead. The Zulus suddenly come to a halt, and throwing a spear into the ground, begin banging another one against their shields, as they stand their ground.

Bromhead: Fire! Reload! Fire! Reload! Independent fire at will!

Owen (to Thomas): That's very nice of him.

Now if I was a Zulu, and my name was Will, I would be a little anxious at this moment.

The falling Zulus in the front row are quickly replaced by the warriors behind them, as the garrison keeps up a steady volley. The Zulus are being hit by fire from the ramparts and both buildings which is correct.

The shocked Zulus do some serious overacting here as they clutch their chests and drop to the ground, but remember, they were trained by watching Laurel and Hardy films. They were not real actors, and as apartheid was still very strong, they were not paid as much as the white actors by order of the government. To keep them happy, Stanley Baker gave them 300 head of cattle.

Hitch: They're just standing there asking for it.

Allen: Keep firing soldier. Mark your targets before you fire.

Bromhead: Adendorff, what's wrong with them? Why don't they fight?

Adendorff: They're counting your guns.

Chard: What?

Adendorff: Can't you see that old boy up on the hill? He's counting your guns. Testing you firing power with the lives of his warriors.

This was certainly not the case at Rorkes Drift. On a signal the Zulus fall back, and Owen starts to lead the men in joyous celebration, as if the battle was won.

Chard (to Adendorff):   Well?
Adendorff: They'll be back.
Chard: Stand fast!

With that command the singing and cheering stops.

Bromhead: Sixty, we dropped at least sixty, wouldn't you say?
Adendorff: Well, that leaves only 3,940.

The first shots were aimed at Hitch on the storehouse roof. The Zulus charged in absolute silence, with their shields held away from their bodies, thus distracting the soilders aim, using every bit of cover to hide themselves. Assistant Commissary Dunne said they were, "A black mass coming on without a sound at a steady trot" and Private Waters said they were, "Forming a line in skirmishing order, just as British soldiers would do".

Chard gave the order to fire at 500 yards, and at 450 yards the men had settled and were shooting calmly and accurately. A sick artillery man named Howard said, "Our firing was very quick, and when struck by the bullets, the niggers would give a spring in the air and fall flat down".

Private James Dunbar here excelled. Shooting from 500–600 yards, he shot 8 Zulus and an Induna off his grey horse, who was alongside Prince Dabulamanzi. This was confirmed by Private Hook in his report in Norman Holme's, "The Silver Wreath", in which he claims, Dunbar shot 9 Zulus and the Induna. Chard later mentioned Dunbar in a letter to Queen Victoria.

Dabulamanzi having witnessed the death of one of his Indunas, dismounted and took shelter behind a tree, leaving him in no position to co-ordinate the attacks, which evolved into frontal assaults on the front wall.

So the first charge has been repulsed and back in the storehouse a drunken Witt is shouting.

Witt: Rise up, my love, my fair one, and come away. Behold, thou art fair, my love!
Chard: How long?
Adendorff: Ten, fifteen minutes. Maybe less, as soon as they've regrouped.

It was a custom of the Zulus to take snuff from the witch doctors before attacking and in a documentary on Islandlwana which was shown on television in 2008, it was proved that the snuff contained cannabis. This I believe made them feel invincible to the bullets as they charged forward, but when it came to hand to hand fighting and facing the bayonet, the reality seemed to set in.

Meanwhile, Witt is continuing with his drunken tirade.

Witt:	Thy lips are like a thread of scarlet, and thy speech is comely.
Bromhead:	He can't be!
Chard:	He is. Drunk as a lord. 15 minutes.
Adendorff:	If we're lucky.

Chard calls for Colour Sergeant Bourne, as in the background Witt can still be heard.

Bourne:	Yes sir, the gentleman has a bottle.
Chard:	Then get him out of here. Put him on his cart. Tie him on if necessary. The sooner we get rid of them the better.
Bourne:	Sir.
Bromhead:	Chard, they won't stand a chance with the Zulus.
Chard:	They're Witt's parishioners aren't they?
Bromhead:	But the woman, do you want to see her killed?
Chard:	Do you, Bromhead? Because you will if you don't get them out of here.

Colour Sergeant Bourne goes to the storehouse to collect Witt.

Bourne: Come along, sir. That's a good gentleman.

Witt slumps to the floor and Bourne turns to the two soldiers with him.

Bourne:	Alright, pick him up.
Witt (groaning):	I have sinned against heaven and before thee.

Bourne grabs Witt's bottle and smashes it on the floor, as Sergeant Windridge is bringing Margareta over from the hospital. Seeing her father being led away, she rushes over to him.

Witt:	Oh, peace be within thy walls.
Margareta:	Father!

Margareta gets on the buggy with her father.

Chard:	Keep driving with the sun at your back. You should make it safely.
Witt:	Sergeant!
Margareta:	Father!
Witt:	Leave me alone!
Chard:	Try to understand him, Miss Witt.
Witt:	Death awaits you. You have made a covenant with death, and with hell you are in agreement. You're all going to die! Don't you realise? Can't you see? You're all going to die!

Chard slaps one of the horses, as Witt continues shouting from the back of the buggy.

Witt:	Die! Death awaits you all!
Private (who guarded Witt):	He's right.
Witt:	Die!
Private:	Why is it us? Why us?
Bourne:	Because we're here lad, and nobody else. Just us.
Chard:	Colour Sergeant.
Bourne:	Right, now get back to your posts. At the double.

The Witt's buggy moves out and the Zulus hidden in the bush rise, but are signalled to go back down and let the Witts' pass.

Brilliant acting by Jack Hawkins, but as a young boy watching the film for the first time, I was glad to see the back of him and his daughter.

SCENE 8 – HERE THEY COME AGAIN

As Chard walks across the compound, note the large box with 24th printed on, this of course refers to the 24th regiment and there certainly aren't many references made to them.

He tries to load his revolver with a trembling hand. A cry of, "Here they come again", pierces the silence.

Bromhead: Volley! Fire!

As the defendants fire, the Zulus duck down en masse.

Owen: I can't see a bloody one now.
Thomas: They've gone to ground.
Owen: Oh.

Hidden Zulus now raise their rifles and go to take up position on the Oksberg hill at a range of about 400 yards, to fire down onto the garrison.

Windridge: There they go.

Although the enemy could not be seen hiding in the bush, shots were fired, which no doubt resulted in the high number of cartridges spent. This could have been down to a trigger finger, as now the Udolko regiment of 41 year olds and Cetewayo's old regiment, the 45 year olds of the Uthulwana regiment, arrive at the scene. Back in the film.

Chard: What the devil's going on? Well, tell me what's happening. I've got to know.

Bromhead:	There on both sides. We haven't enough men at the north wall.
Adendorff:	Can't you take some from the south?
Chard:	How will we hold that if we do? Damn it Adendorff, you're supposed to know. Are they going to hit us everywhere at once?.
Adendorff:	I told you, remember? The horns of the buffalo. The south could have been a feint. We can't man the whole perimeter. We've got to outgun them somewhere, right?
Chard:	Alright, Bromhead. Take men from the south, one section in three. Reinforce the north wall.
Bromhead:	But if they do come up from the south again?
Chard:	Get on with it Mr. Bromhead. At the double.
Bromhead:	Colour Sergeant Bourne. I want every other man from sections 1, 3 and 5 over at the north wall.
Adendorff:	Where would you like me?
Chard:	You pick your own ground. It's your country isn't it?

Chard puts his last bullet into his revolver, and his hand is now steady.

In truth, Dabulamanzi ordered simultaneous assaults on both walls as the light was fading at about 6 p.m.

In the film, the Zulus have taken up position on Oskarberg hill, ready to fire down into the garrison, and a shot rings out.

Hitch:	Hey, who left the door open?

As Hitch ducks down, his helmet falls off and he puts it back on the wrong way round. Heavy fire now pours down from Oskarberg hill.

Bromhead:	Blazes! Where did they get those?
Adendorff:	I'd say off the bodies of your regiment at Islandlwana.
Bromhead:	Well that's a bitter pill, our own damn rifles.

This is a great myth that the Zulus were armed with the rifles looted at Islandlwana. At this time, the victorious Zulus would still be in the act of looting and mutilation of the dead soldiers. However, as the fleeing fugitives ran for their lives from the battlefield, I imagine the first thing they discarded was their rifle, which surely would have hindered their movement, then belts holding their ammunition pouches. Also, stampeding pack mules would have shed their loads of equipment, which surely included boxes of ammunition. All of this would have been collected by the chasing Zulus, so I believe they had some Martini-Henry rifles, but how many I don't know.

But the reserves did have some rifles from men killed at Islandlwana, when they ran into Second Lieutenant Edward Dyson's section, who had been ordered to hold a high position, about 500 yards from the main camp.

Fighting to the last man, 20 year old Dyson and his men were annihilated and most certainly lost their weapons to the enemy.

In December, 1936, Colour Sergeant Bourne made a BBC radio broadcast on which he said, "The Zulus had collected the rifles from the men they had killed at Islandlwana, and had captured the ammunition from the mules, which had stampeded and threw their loads, so our own arms were used against us".

So the Zulus have some stolen rifles, and they also had been receiving smuggled guns across the Natal border and through Portuguese Mozambique for about 30 years. However, most were old weapons, including the Brown Bess flintock of the Napoleonic wars, which only had a range of about 100 yards.

Another problem was the Zulus were short of ammunition and were forced to make their own using pebbles and bits of iron, which obviously did not shoot like a British cartridge. But when your being shot at there is always the danger of being hit.

Bourne:	Keep your heads down.
Chard:	Corporal Allen!
Allen:	Sir!
Chard:	This your section now? Well see if you can keep the head's of those marksmen down.
Allen:	Can't see none of 'em, sir.
Chard:	You should know Corporal Allen, fire at the smoke, keeps them pinned down, not us.

Gunfire is exchanged as Chard walks along the line.

Chard:	Mr.Bromhead!
Bromhead:	Not the best of shots are they?
Chard:	Get a platoon together.
Bromhead:	I'll need more than one old boy, if I'm going up there after them.

Chard: You're not going up there after them. Get a platoon of good bayonet men. Take them head on anything that breaks through when our lines are weaken.

Bromhead: Oh! It's still a holding action is it?

Chard: That's right. Your job is to plug the gaps from the inside, and get yourself a good sergeant.

Bromhead: Yes, sir.

Bromhead removes his sword and takes up a rifle and bayonet with sergeant Windridge.

Taking off his helmet, Hitch climbs on top of the mealie bag barricade to get a better shot.

Allen: Hitch! Get down!

Hitch: How can I shoot them if I can't see them.

Suddenly Hitch is hit and screams out.

Hitch: My leg! Corp!

In Hitch's account in Norman Holme's, "The Silver Wreath", he says that Private Deakin (It was actually Deacon), said to him, "Fred, when it comes to the last shall I shoot you?" Hitch replied, "No, they have very nearly done for me and they can finish me right off when it comes to the last".

Private Hitch was actually hit in the right shoulder, shattering his shoulder blade. Surgeon Reynolds removed 39 pieces of broken bone from his shoulder. Another soldier ripped the lining of his jacket and bound it round the injured Hitch, who, armed with Bromhead's revolver, continued to fight on. He later handed out ammunition with Corporal Allen, like in the film, until he passed out through lack of blood, and woke up the next morning. His actions won him the Victoria Cross.

Bromhead, on seeing the wounded Hitch said, "Mate, I am sorry to see you down."

Bromhead must have been his mate, because he visited him regularly whilst he was recovering after the battle.

It is also worth mentioning that earlier in the battle, a Zulu was in the act of assegaiing Bromhead, when Hitch trained his empty rifle at him, forcing him to duck down and hop away.

The excellent comradeship between officers and men continued after the battle, when Private Bush, who was covered in blood from a wound to the nose, shared his dirty towel with Chard, as they washed their faces in a muddy pool of water.

In the film, as Allen goes to help Hitch, he is shot in his right upper body, and falls back pulling Hitch with him.

Meanwhile we see the first British casualty, the private who was standing guard at the storeroom, who we later discover is called Cole, played by Gary Bond. He is shot in the neck and falls down as maize from a bullet hole in the mealie bags pours across his face and into his mouth.

Private Thomas Cole, nicknamed "Old King", was shot through the head, splattering his brains all around. His number was 801 and he served in "B" Company, after attesting at Monmouth on 23/3/76 aged 20 years 10 months. Chard mentioned him in his report and he is buried in the cemetery at Rorkes Drift.

Now, back to the film again and Corporal Allen's bullet wound has mysteriously moved from his right side to his left. Hitch lies injured under Allen.

Hitch: Can I undo my tunic button now, can I corp?

Allen reaches over and manages to undo one before he collapses onto Hitch's legs, causing him to cry out in agony. Across comes Colour Sergeant Bourne, who drags Allen up.

Bourne: Stretcher bearers!

Bourne moves away as two hospital orderlies rush over to help.

Actually killed at this time, was a Private Edward Nicholas, shot through the head. His number was 625 and he served in "B" company, after attesting at Newport on 30/7/75, aged 18 years and is buried with his comrades at Rorkes Drift. On official documents, he is wrongly named as Nicholls.

On a lighter note, Reverend Smith was moving amongst the men handing out ammunition, complaining about the bad language coming from the soldiers. Going to one man he said, "Please my good man stop that cussing. We may shortly have to answer for our sins."

The reply was, "Alright minister, you do the praying and I will send the black bastards to hell as fast as I can".

For his bravery during the battle handing out the ammunition, he earned the nickname "Ammunition Smith".

I recently visited his grave in Preston cemetery, where a red marble headstone marks his final resting place. The top reads "To live in hearts we leave behind is not to die," and the final words are "He was a brave and modest christian gentleman".

Two more casualties, both shot dead at this time, were Privates 1335 James Chick and 1051 John Scanlon, both buried at the battlefield.

As the Zulus reached the barricades, they repeatedly tried to grab the soldiers rifles by the muzzle, so they could thrust with their assegais in the traditional upward manner.

One Zulu succeeded and had hold of the rifle of a corporal of the Army Hospital Corps, who he was about to spear, when Dalton shot him.

Chard recalled from his second report, "Each time as the attack was repulsed by us, the Zulus close to us seemed to vanish in the bush, those some little distance off keeping up a fire all the time.

Then, as if moved by a single impulse, they rose up in the bush as thick as possible, rushing madly up to the wall, (some of them being already close to it), seizing where they could, the muzzles of our men's rifles, or their bayonets, and attempting to use their assegais and to get over the wall. A rapid rattle of fire from our rifles, stabs with the bayonets, and in a few moments the Zulus were driven back, disappearing in the bush as before, and keeping up their fire".

Hook stated, "The Zulus were swarming around us, and there was an extraordinary rattle as the bullets struck the biscuits boxes and queer thumps as they plumped into the bags of mealies."

He also said of Dalton, "He was one of the bravest men that ever lived".

Surgeon Reynolds reported, "Here and there a black body doubled up, and went writhing and bouncing into the dust, but the great host came steadily on, spreading out, spreading out, spreading out till they seemed like a giant pair of nutcrackers opening around the little nuts of Rorkes Drift.

It was nasty, really nasty, the inevitability of that silent mass closing in upon us".

A great problem facing the garrison was that the Zulus had plenty of natural cover to conceal themselves behind, particularly the orchard and garden, which had not been cleared.

Reynolds said of it, "It was a frightful oversight, the leaving of that garden and shrubbery.

Heavens! They rained lead on us at the distance of a cricket pitch or two".

Time and time again the Zulus attacked with assegais and knobkerries and were repulsed by bayonet and rifle butt in bloody hand to hand fighting, with each man fighting for his life.

I believe the comradeship shown by the defenders, against a fanatical foe, served them well in their darkest hour, and eventually won them the day.

During these tense moments, corporal Schiess jumped on top of the mealie bags on the rocky ledge, and shot and bayoneted several Zulus in an amazing act of bravery, whilst he received a bullet wound to his already injured foot. He was awarded the Victoria Cross for his courage in the defence.

In another lesser act of bravery, Chard's batman, Robson, concentrated his fire on the Zulus who were ransacking the engineer's wagon, which had been left outside the perimeter, claiming it was, "his stuff". Records don't state whether he was a good shot or not.

On the Zulu side, in their thirst for blood, they killed three horses which had been tethered to a tree near the garden wall, which I think is a sign of their growing frustration, but not their bravery.

Corporal Attwood said, "They do not seem to have much fear. They are very daring, coming right up to the guns, such horrid looking brutes, quite naked, except a thong of something about their loins".

Attwood also wrote to his father saying, "I made an awful mess of one fellow. He was running towards the house in a slightly sloping position when I let fly at him and struck him in the crown of the head, the effect of which was to blow the entire side of his face away. I was at an upper window, the only one in the barn I call it".

He was in fact shooting from the storehouse with good effect.

The Zulu fire was also finding it's target as Corporal Scammell of the NNC was hit in the back. Falling to the ground, he called out for some water and was attended to by Acting Commissariat Louis Byrne. Just as Byrne opened his water bottle and bent down to give Scammell a drink, he was shot dead and fell on top of the injured Scammell. The corporal struggled free and crawled over to Chard to hand him his cartridges, before reporting to surgeon Reynolds. Unlike the film, Chard was using a Martini-Henry rifle as was Bromhead.

Like in the film, Bromhead, with a squad of good bayonet men, repulsed the Zulu charges, and it shows the character of this "officer and gentleman", that when the going got tough, he was, "One of the lads".

The time is now 6pm and with casualties mounting, Chard decided to withdraw to the line of biscuit boxes, leaving the defenders and patients in the hospital isolated, and the Zulus immediately took up position behind the deserted front wall.

SCENE 9 – ATTACK, DAMN YOU!

Chard: Come on, attack, damn you!

The Zulus rise up to attack as the call, "Here they come", is shouted. Chard seems isolated at this moment from the main action.

Chard: North wall, volley fire! Present! At 100 yards. Fire! Reload! Independent fire at will.

Fierce hand to hand fighting ensues as the Zulus quickly reach the barricades. Colour Sergeant Bourne is seen leading by example, using the bayonet to good effect. Scheiss, looking from the hospital decides it's time he took part. Bromhead leads a squad of men to plug the gaps as he was truly ordered to do in scene 8 by Chard. As the Zulus storm over the mealie bags, Scheiss stumbles as he leaves the hospital and struggles on one knee to fasten his bandage which has come undone. Still on one knee, he bayonets then shoots another Zulu as the garrison seems overrun. In the background, a colonial carrying a box is shot and falls down. Judging by his acting, he must have been watching the same films as the Zulu cast. Chard goes over to him as Zulus dash forward.

Now, this colonial was also carrying a rifle on his left shoulder without a bayonet. He falls down with it still on his shoulder, but when Chard picks it up, it is conveniently propped up against the mealie bags, with a bayonet attached.

Chard shoots one charging Zulu with the last bullet in his revolver and picks up the rifle with bayonet and swings it butt first at another two Zulus who have him cornered. Spinning the rifle the right way round, Chard knocks one of the Zulus to the ground, but is floored by the other. As the Zulu stands over Chard to finish him off with his assegai, his thrust is blocked by Scheiss' crutch, who duly bayonets the Zulu.

Scheiss: Mr. Chard, I'll get you help.

Scheiss fights his way through the swarming Zulus as Chard tries to drag himself away. Bromhead sees Chard in trouble.

Bromhead: Keep our squad at the wall, Sergeant.

He then rushes over to Chard. Note the wagon, not overturned as they were earlier, when Witt was requesting them so he could take the sick away. It is upright, with mealie bags on top and barrels underneath, which was how the real two wagons would have looked.

Bromhead: Chard! Are you alright?
Chard: Take……command.

Chard is bleeding from a wound under his left ear.

Bromhead: Corporal.
Chard: You're the professional. Take command.

Bromhead calls for the Lance Corporal.

Bromhead (to Chard): Now, listen old boy, your not badly hurt. We need you! Damn you, we need you. Understand?

He then shouts to the Lance Corporal.

Bromhead: Get him to surgeon Reynolds.
Chard: Take command. You want it, don't you?
Bromhead: Sergeant Windridge!
Windridge: Sir!

On reaching the hospital, the Lance Corporal leaves Chard at the doorway. Looking in Chard can see Reynolds operating on Private Cole, who we heard about in scene 8, on a blood stained table.

Reynolds: Scalpel.

Reynolds looks up and glares at Chard.

Reynolds: Orderly, damn it! Will you keep the flies away! Fan it! Damn you, Chard! Damn all you butchers.

Private Cole lifts himself up from the table.

Cole: Why? Why? Why?

This sounds like the cue to another Tom Jones song.

Reynolds: It's alright boy, you sleep. I'm damned if I can tell you why.

Reynolds looks to an orderly.

Reynolds: You know this boy?

Reynolds puts his ear to Cole's chest.

Orderly: Name of Cole, sir. He was a paper hanger.
Reynolds: Well, he's a dead paper hanger now.

Reynolds walks over to Chard in his blood splattered apron.

Reynolds: Are you alright?

Chard falls forward and Reynolds grabs hold of him.
    The battle along the barricades continues and on a signal the Zulus retreat.

Soldier: There they go boys. After 'em!

As he goes to climb over the mealie bags, he is pulled back by Colour Sergeant Bourne.

Bourne: Stand fast! They're retiring, sir.
Bromhead: North wall hold your fire.

Shots rain down as Bourne shouts, "Down!"

Bromhead: What is it now? Another blasted trick?

Soldier:	They're forming up on the South plain again sir.
Bromhead:	I knew it! I knew it! They're going to attack both walls at once.
Adendorff:	I doubt it, not unless they have no other choice, anyhow. It would mean the old general couldn't use his rifles on the hillside for fear of hitting down onto his own men. This way he keeps probing for weaknesses on the one wall, while he keeps the other one pinned down.
Bromhead:	Oh, yes.

On a signal the Zulus attack the South wall again.

Windridge:	They're on the move, sir!
Bromhead:	North wall, keep those rifle men on the hillside pinned down. South wall, volley fire! Present! Fire! Reload!

Back in the hospital, Hook is still playing find the bullet, with his three tin cups.

Private:	Hookie, come on boy, do something!
Hook:	I'm excused duty.
Private:	Well I haven't excused you, have I?
Hook:	Ah, you want some help, why didn't you say so?

Hook leaps up, grabs his rifle and using the butt end, smashes a window, and turning the rifle round he fires his first shot.
    Meanwhile, Dalton and the cook are handing out ammunition, and both are shouldering rifles.

Cook:	This rifle sir! Honestly, I cant manage it.
Dalton:	Now, now, you heard what the officer said. Come on.
Cook:	But if it really came down to it, sir, I couldn't really shoot anyone.

Dalton suddenly cries out as a Zulu leaps on top of the barricade.

Dalton:	Careful! Pop that chap somebody.

Dalton did shout out these very words. The film is spot on here. Dalton had already shot a Zulu who was about to spear a man of the Army Hospital Corps, when he cried out the warning. The Zulu is shot and falls on top of the mealie bags and is pushed off by the soldier who shot him.

Dalton: Good fellow. Good fellow.

As Dalton turns, he is shot in the back and as cook kneels down to check on him, a Zulu spear crashes into his back and he falls over Dalton's legs. Dalton manages to slip from under the dead cook and crawls over to the ammunition box.

The film has it right again about Dalton. He was hit near the shoulder, with the bullet passing straight through him, and he was taken to surgeon Reynolds.

The Zulus were keeping up tremendous assaults and Colour Sergeant Bourne was so moved by them that he wrote in his report, "To show their fearlessness and their contempt for the redcoats and small numbers, they tried to leap the parapet, and at times seized our bayonets, only to be shot down. Looking back, one cannot but admire their bravery".

Bourne, who was awarded the Distinguished Conduct Medal and an annuity of £10, the same as awarded to the Victoria Cross, was also awarded a commission, which he declined due to the expense involved as an officer. During the battle he moved among the men and said of them, "Not for one moment did they flinch, their courage and their bravery cannot be expressed in words, for me they were an example all my soldiering days".

Reynolds is treating Chard in the hospital, while soldiers are firing from inside through loop holes.

Reynolds (to Chard):   You're doing fine.
Chard: Where……?
Reynolds: You want to rest here a bit?

Chard doesn't answer and gets up and leaves. Sitting outside are the wounded Allen and Hitch.

Hitch: Watch it!
Allen: Can you move your leg?
Hitch: If you want me to dance.
Allen: I want you to crawl. Come on you slovenly soldier, we've got work to do.

Together they hobble away and find Dalton slumped by his ammunition box.

Allen: It's alright sir, we'll do that for you.
Dalton: I'm alright.
Allen: You'd better get to the surgeon sir. I'll try to get someone to help you.
Dalton: I can manage.

Together, which is true as stated in scene 8, Allen and Hitch dragged the ammunition box round he defenders, on their hands and knees. It is surely this self sacrifice and comradeship, which won the day for the men of the 24th, against overwhelming odds.

Chard has steadied himself and is ready to go back into action. Bromhead is leading his men on the barricade.

Bromhead: Hold them! Hold them!

Privates Owen and Thomas are firing from a upturned wagon as the Zulus form up again for another charge. Looking up at this awesome sight is Private Hitch.

Hitch: Oh, my God!
Chard: Bromhead, reorganise your flying platoon with Sergeant Windridge.
Bromhead: But I …… yes, sir, of course.

A corporal brings over Chard's revolver.

Chard: Well done, corporal. Stand by.
Corporal: Sir.

The Zulu leaders are positioned on top of a hill to organise the attacks, whilst at this time Dabulamanzi was concealed behind a tree.

Chard: Colour Sergeant Bourne.
Bourne: Sir! Are you alright, sir?
Chard: Thank you, Mr Bourne. The men on the church roof, have them support your fire against the hillside.

Chard: Corporal!
Corporal: Sir!
Bourne: Section on the roof, bring your rifles about on the hillside. Fire at the smoke.

Chard (to the corporal): The men on the hospital loopholes. They've nothing to fire at. Bring them to the front windows to support the north wall. Colour Sergeant.

Bourne: Sir!
Chard: I want half your men, now.
Bourne: An even number, sir?
Chard: Form two lines on the double.
Bourne: Sir!

Given their signal from the hillside, the Zulus move forward again.

SCENE 10 – VOLLEY FIRE!

Bourne:		Company! Company! En garde!

As the Zulus reach the barricades, the order is given.

Chard:		Fall back!

The Zulus smash their way through the mealie bags, whilst Bourne has his men ready for the onslaught.

Bourne:		Clear the line of fire.
Chard:		Front rank! Fire! Rear rank! Fire!

As the front rank fire, they kneel down and the rear rank fire and move through them. They then kneel and reload and the rear rank fire and move forward. This action is repeated so that there is a continual volley of fire from a line of soldiers, moving forward all the time.
	This stops the Zulus, who are taking heavy casualties and they are forced to retreat. As the defenders rush forward the order,"Independent fire at will" is given.

Chard:		Cease firing.

Zulu bodies litter the ground as the orderlies bring out buckets of water.

Owen:		Hey, Thomas. There's some water.
Thomas:		Oh, thank god.

They both hurriedly dip a cup into the bucket to quench their thirst.

Thomas:	470 Davies was hit, you know?
Owen:	No!
Thomas:	Aye, in the throat.
Owen:	What a pity. The man is a great bass baritone. In the throat is it?
Thomas:	Aye.

There was a Private 470 Davies. He was attested at Wrexham aged 21 years old and posted to the 2/24th on 4/12/74. He certainly took part in the defence of Rorkes Drift, but he certainly was not killed in action. There is no trace of him in the regimental records after 4/3/81, and it is presumed he was discharged around this time.

In the film, Thomas gets up to go.

Owen:	Where are you going?
Thomas:	I'm going to see that calf, man.
Owen:	Hey, come back you fool. What are you doing? Tommy!

The men are working on the final redoubt.

There was in fact a huge pile of mealie bags which Chard ordered to be hollowed out in the middle for the wounded, and used as an elevated firing position, for the last stand.

Chard:	Mr. Bourne, there should be twelve more men working on this redoubt.
Bourne:	There very tired, sir.
Chard:	I don't give a damn, and I want this nine foot high, firing steps inside. Form details to clear away the Zulu warriors. Rebuild the south ramparts. Keep them moving. You understand?
Bourne:	Yes, sir. Very good, sir. Alright lads, keep it moving.

It was essential for Chard to keep the men active, because tired as they were, he could not afford to let them rest, for fear of going into a deep sleep. He had to keep them alert for the next attack, which was already forming up.

The man Chard actually gave the order to construct the redoubt was Commissary Walter Dunne. Dunne was a quiet man, who had served in the

Ninth Cape Frontier War, and he personally supervised the construction of the redoubt, while under fire from Zulus all around.

Work was stopped when a voice yelled that he could see marching redcoats approaching from Helpmekaar. As the rumour spread, a mighty cheer rang out, which confused the Zulus, who halted their next attack for a short while.

Chard wrote, "It is very strange that this report should have arisen amongst us, for the two companies, 24th regiment from Helpmekaar did come down to the foot of the hill, but not, I believe, in sight of us. They marched back to Helpmekaar on the report of Rorkes Drift having fallen".

Spalding, as we know, had left for Helpmekaar earlier, and again he let his command down. He was close enough to see the burning flames of the hospital roof, but he also saw a large group of Zulu skirmishers. He now had a big decision to make. Does he go forward to relieve his men pinned in their tiny garrison, or return to Helpmekaar? This very careful man, some might say coward, retreated and formed a defensive laager, preparing for an attack which never materialised.

SCENE 11 – ATTACK ON THE BLIND SPOT

The blind spot refers to the hospital, which was the weak link in the defences. However, in truth, the Zulus had been fiercely attacking this position from the very start.

Hook, in the hospital, described the position as, "Pinned like rats in a hole".

Hook: We're next boys, this is the blind spot. Even if those flaming officers ain't seen it, I bet the Zulus have.

Hook goes back to his three tin cup trick.

Hook: Come on Howarth, put your money up.

There was no one of that name at Rorkes Drift.

Howarth: Have you gone stupid? What bloody good do you think it will do you if you do win? We're all goners!
Hook: Well, it doesn't matter if you lose, does it?

Hook knocks the cups flying in temper.

Hook: Hughsie, there's some, er, brandy in Reynolds medical cabinet, go and borrow some.
Hughes: It's locked up down that end.
Hook: Kick it down then.

Private: Hey, that's company punishment.

Hook (laughing): Company punishment.

Maxfield: On the right. Form close columns of platoons. By the right.

Hook: You lucky bastard!

Meanwhile, Thomas has gone over to see the calf and finds it lying dead.

Thomas: Oh dear, oh dear. Well your mum will need somebody to milk her now, won't she?

The Zulus are signalled forward again to attack.

Bourne: Stand to!

Thomas: Alright, alright, I can hear you.

He steps over the dead calf and closes the kraal gate behind him, but does not lock it properly, and the gate swings slightly open.
 Regarding the cattle, I have found no evidence of any being present.
 The Zulus attack in force and head for the hospital as Hook predicted, and some scramble onto the roof.
 Chard is firing up at them with his revolver as Bromhead gets a lift up onto the storehouse roof, armed with a rifle and bayonet.
 Up on the roof, a soldier is shot in the back and a rising Zulu is also shot. The Zulus furiously make a hole in the thatched roof of the hospital with their spears. A private fires up at them as the man by his side is struck by a spear in the chest.
 A Zulu drops through the hole in the roof and is about to spear an unarmed soldier when Hook turns and shoots him, saving the soldier's life.

Hook: Out you get, Hookie. You've done your bit.

Hook puts on his tunic, which he was reluctant to do earlier, when ordered by Maxfield.
 The Zulus are swarming outside the hospital as Hook leaves the room, and he sees the outside door being smashed in, and spears pointing through it. Panic stricken, he darts back inside.

Hook: Quick! Thousands of 'em! 612!

There is no record of number 612, which is surprising, because the film has other soldiers numbered correctly.

Hook pulls a double bunk bed across the door, just as the Zulus break through the outside door and start battering at the door Hook is now defending. The Zulus are suffering casualties from fire from inside the hospital and from the soldiers now entrenched behind the biscuit boxes.

Hook: Knock a hole in that wall!

This is true, and the men dig at the wall with their bayonets. They would also have used pick axes from the engineer's wagon as well.

Shots are fired up at the Zulus on the roof, and the thatched roof catches fire from a flash from one of the soldier's rifles.

This is not true, as the Zulus eventually managed to fire the damp roof with flaming spears.

The men in the hospital were now in even greater danger as smoke filled the tiny rooms and Hook later said, "It meant that we were either to be massacred or burned alive, or get out of the building. To get out seemed impossible, for if we left the hospital by the only door which had been left open, we should instantly fall into the midst of the Zulu".

Bromhead, with a few men are firing at the Zulus on the hospital roof from their position on the storehouse roof and Bromhead knocks a Zulu down, sending him crashing to the ground.

Windridge: Better get down now, sir. Sir, get down now, sir.

Bromhead seems obsessed and is shooting down with his revolver with good success.

In the hospital, the Zulus are trying to break a door down, as a soldier crawls through a knocked out hole, into the safety of the next room. As he does so, 593 Jones in the other room is standing on guard, ready to bayonet anyone who pops their head through.

Soldier: No! Jones. It's me!
593 Jones: Come on, get through you bloody Englishman!

The wounded are being carried through the hole in the wall, as a burning beam comes crashing down, setting the place alight.

Hook: Get out! Get out! Get out!

Colour Sergeant Bourne's headstone in Beckenham Cemetery,
Elmer's End Road, Kent

Nigel Green as
Colour Sergeant Bourne

Private Hook played by James Booth plays find the bullet, ignorant of the impending danger

Colour Sergeant Bourne goes to take away the Reverend Witt, played by Jack Hawkins, as he tries hopelessly to overturn the wagons

Lieutenant Chard, played by Stanley Baker restrains Margareta Witt, played by Ulla Jacobsson

Here I am holding Chard's revolver in the arsenal at the Royal Engineer's Museum, Chatham, Kent

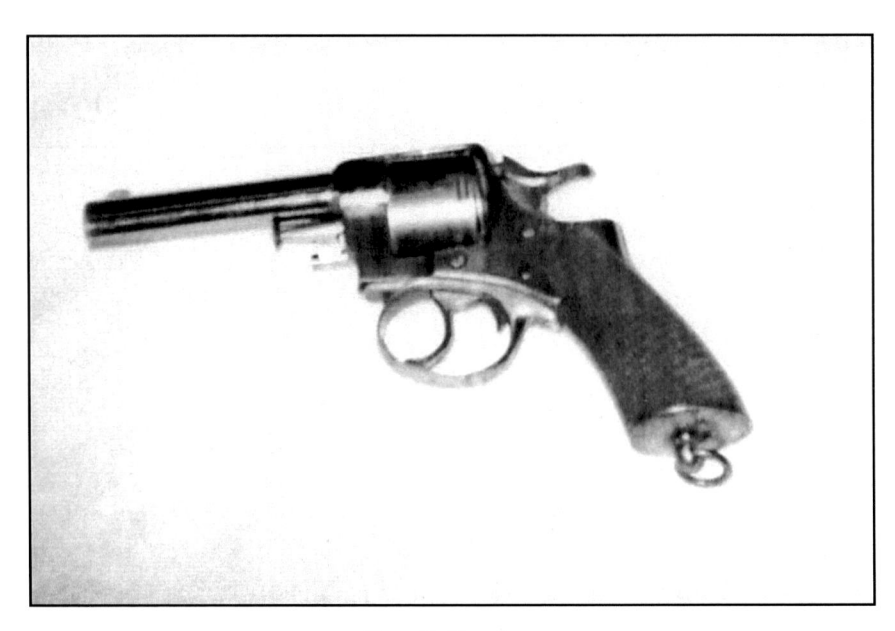

Chard's Revolver

Chard fires his revolver up at the Zulus as the fighting intensifies

A Sergeant shoots a Zulu armed with a rifle on the storehouse roof

Lieutenant Bromhead, played by Michael Caine, gives the order to fire as the film reaches it's climax

Dead Zulus litter the ground as the final assault is halted at point blank range

Heavy fighting as the defender's make their last stand

Chard can't believe the Zulus have returned, as Adendorff, played by
Gert Van Den Bergh looks on

The headstone of Victoria Cross recipient, Private Williams Jones, who is buried in a public grave at Phillip Park Cemetery, in Manchester

Hook is holding the door alone, with his body pressed against the bunk bed. He fires through the door and backs through the hole into the next room. A Zulu quickly follows him through the hole and is grabbed by Hook.

Hook: Jonesy!

593 Jones immediately bayonets the Zulu in the back with a swift thrust, as the building burns fiercely.

We are now seeing the real Hook, fighting to save the lives of the sick, with no consideration for his own safety, actions which earned him the Victoria Cross.

The men are struggling through the burning building as more beams come crashing down around them. They head up the stairs, and at the top is a ladder which they climb down to the relative safety of the ground below.

Chard is stood at the bottom, checking who is still fit to fight and who needs to go to Reynolds. Smoke is now bellowing out of the hospital as the men hurry down the ladder. Chard is checking each man individually, their faces blackened by the smoke.

Chard: Get to surgeon Reynolds. Right, on the wall.

During this intense part of the battle, two privates thought they could outwit the Zulus. They were Privates John Waters and William Beckett. Waters told an account of it, which was published in the Cambrian newspaper in June 1879.

Waters was special orderly in the hospital, and he and Beckett hid in a cupboard as the Zulus charged into their room in the hospital. Waters claimed he killed many of them, but then had to leave because of the suffocating smoke. He put on a black robe which he found in the cupboard, presumably one of Witt's and ran outside and hid in the long grass. The Zulus must have thought him a dead comrade, as they passed by him and some even trod on him. Beckett was not so lucky. He had fled the hospital 30 minutes earlier and was immediately stabbed through his stomach and fell in a ditch. He was still alive the next morning, but Reynolds could not save the poor fellow.

Waters stated in his account that when he got up at day break, he had expected every minute of his life to be his last, and on seeing his comrades said, "Thank god, I have got my life". He nearly didn't, because on seeing him with his blackened face and black robe, his comrades nearly shot him, thinking he was a Zulu.

Hook was lucky too, for as he bravely fought on, he was struck by a spear on the front of his helmet, leaving only a scalp wound, which did not bother him.

In the film, Hook is fighting off the Zulus single handed as the delirious Maxfield shouts from his bed.

Maxfield: Hook! I know you!
Hook: What about the money you sent my old woman?
Maxfield: Hook!

Hook fights his way back, when he could easily have left.

Maxfield: That's it, Hook, my lad!

Hook drops his rifle, and struggling with a Zulu, he grabs hold of his assegai as his friend pops his head through a hole in the wall, and shoots the Zulu in the back. Maxfield begins to struggle across the room.

Hook: Stay where you are, Maxfield!

Hook's friend calls for him to ,"Get out", as he defiantly continues defending the hole into his room.

Maxfield (laughing):   That's my boy, Hook! You're a solider now! I've made a soldier of you!

The room is filling up with smoke, as Hook searches for Maxfield.

Hook: Where's my bloody sergeant?

Through the fire and the smoke, a Zulu enters and is about to stab the defenceless Maxfield, when the burning roof comes crashing down on them both.

In truth the delirious Maxfield was stabbed to death in his bed, when he refused all attempts to move him, and reluctantly he had to be left by his comrades. This was an action which Hook always regretted.

Back in the film, unable to do anything, Hook backs off through the loophole, as the last of the men climb down the ladder to Chard.

At this time, a Xhosa native was also left behind. He was questioned by the Zulus then, assegaied in his bed.

Chard is still checking the men as they descend from the blazing hospital.

Chard: Is everyone out? On the wall.

Hughes: Hookie? Where's Hookie? Hookie! Come down, Hookie!

One of his friends climbs back up the ladder to find him. Meanwhile, Hook is making his way to the stairs, but stops at the medicine cabinet and smashes the glass on it with the bloodied Zulu spear he had been fighting with. He reaches inside and grabs hold of a bottle, as his friend yells at him.

Friend: Hookie, that's a flogging offence.

Ignoring the warning, Hook smashes the neck off the bottle and takes a drink.

Friend: Get out, for God's sake, man!

After another swig Hook follows his friend to safety.

Bromhead: Everybody out?
Chard: Everybody that will get out. Abandon the outside ramparts.
Bromhead: Bugler! Retire to this wall.

The fire and noise panic the cattle, who break through the unlocked gate and rush in front of the attacking Zulus. Some Zulus are trampled underfoot by the frightened cattle, who have now formed a barrier between the frustrated Zulus, and the defendants standing firm behind their mealie bags. Again the Zulus are forced to withdraw and regroup.

Chard: Colour Sergeant, carry on building the inner redoubt.
Bourne: Sir! Alright, nobody told you to stop working!

Hook offers the best account for the fight for the hospital, which originally appeared in the Royal Magazine for February, 1905. He was in a room with 9 sick men when he heard Private John Williams shout, "The Zulus are swarming all over the place. They've dragged Joseph Williams out and killed him".

John Williams, Joseph Williams and William Horrigan had been defending one of the rooms for more than an hour, until they ran out of ammunition.

As the Zulus burst in, they grabbed Joseph Williams and dragged him outside to his death. Horrigan was also killed, whilst John Williams, managed to knock a hole in the wall and escape through it.

A big Zulu seized Hook's rifle, but he managed to free it, and slipping a cartridge in, he shot the big fellow at point blank range. As Hook defended the doorway single handed, John Williams was getting the sick through the knocked out hole into the next room.

Hook refers to a heavy man he had to drag along called Conley, but I can find no record, perhaps he meant Private 906 John Connolly. This man had a broken leg, and in Hook's efforts to drag him though a hole, he broke the poor man's leg again.

The last to leave the hospital were Hook, John Williams and Robert and William Jones, and it says a lot of the bravery and self sacrifice of these men, as all four of them received the Victoria Cross.

The sick patients were lowered through a window high up in the wall, then had to cover 40 yards of open ground to Chard's position behind the biscuit boxes. Chard called for two volunteers to assist the patients as they were lowered to the ground. Private Hitch and Allen, both themselves wounded, raced across no-man's land to offer their help, covered by fire from Chard's position. In turn, Hitch and Allen, carried or dragged each patient to safety.

Trooper Hunter of the Natal Mounted Police hesitated and tried to crawl to the biscuit boxes, and was stabbed to death.

Chard said of Hunter, "Dazed by the glare of the burning hospital and the firing that was going on all around, was assegaied before our eyes, the Zulu who killed him immediately afterwards falling". Trooper Hunter, was fortunately the only casualty in the retreat from the hospital to the biscuit boxes.

Reverend Smith said of the patients ordeal, "The window being high up and the Zulus already within the room behind them, each man had a fall in escaping and then had to crawl, (for none of them could walk),through the enemies fire inside the entrenchment".

When reaching the line of biscuit boxes, the wounded were treated by surgeon Reynolds, in the midst of heavy fire and hurled spears.

The battle for the hospital lasted over two hours and the questions must be asked. Why did Chard leave them in such a vulnerable position? And why weren't the holes to communicate between the rooms made earlier? The hospital is now burning away uncontrollably.

Hook: Look at that, do you think he wanted it that way?

Friend: Look at it burn!

Chard (to Bromhead): Anyone in there?

Bromhead shakes his head.

Chard:	Then we'll have to take them from the outside wall.
Bromhead:	Colour Sergeant Bourne!
Bourne:	Sir!

Meanwhile, some of the garrison are trying to get a little rest.

Thomas:	Hey, Owen! Are you awake, man?
Owen:	What is it?
Thomas:	I didn't think it was going to die.
Owen:	Can you see something?
Thomas:	No, the calf, I'm talking about.
Owen:	There's sorry I am.
Thomas:	Aye seems a pity doesn't it?
Owen:	How many times have they come since sunset, do you reckon?
Thomas:	I don't know. Do you think they'll come again?

Shots are fired by the Zulus.

Owen: I think they've got more guts than we have, boyo.

In the hospital, Reynolds calls for "Soldiers", as one of the two men guarding the window in his room is shot, and the other is stabbed. As a Zulu tries to get through the window, a soldier rushes in and shoots the brave warrior and another soldier also comes to help.

Reynolds: Alright, back to your posts. You, hold there. Orderly, see to these men.

The hospital is now totally engulfed in flames and starting to collapse as Hook looks on.
    The film depicts the struggle in the hospital, with it's small, smoked filled rooms brilliantly, with the men hammering at the inner walls, to make them big enough to carry the sick through.
    But, at this time, the Zulus were also attacking the storehouse, and trying to light the roof, but each time they were repulsed.
    They were also camped under the rocky ledge, springing up suddenly to fire at the defenders.

SCENE 12 – DAWN: DAY 2

Chard's position at 7pm, was holding onto the storehouse and the stone kraal.

The burning hospital lit up the sky, and the defenders could identify their targets in the dark as they rushed in. Gunner Howard recalled, "When the flames burst out it was all the better for us, for we could see the Zulus and they could not see us".

As darkness fell, repeated attacks were launched against the stone kraal, forcing the defenders back to the middle, then to the inner wall. The Zulus then held the high, middle wall, but as they popped their heads over, they were blasted at short range by the men behind the inner wall.

The Zulus continued night fighting, which was against their tradition, but the attacks were losing momentum.

In the film, the men are resting as Chard goes over to wake Colour Sergeant Bourne.

Chard: Colour Sergeant, put a third of our men in the redoubt. Send the bugler to me.
Bourne: I was asleep sir.

This poor man is apologising for taking forty winks, and I can honestly imagine the real Bourne saying that.

Bromhead (To Chard): You let me sleep. You shouldn't have done that. Is there any water?
Chard: I sent what was left to Reynolds.
Bromhead: Yes, of course. It's fear dries the mouth, isn't it? When a man's as thirsty as this.
Chard: I could have drunk a river. Thank you for what you said.

Bromhead: Hmmm? Oh, you mean about our needing you? Yes. Don't bother old boy, it's true.

Regarding the water situation, the water cart had been abandoned near the hospital when Chard ordered the retreat to the biscuits boxes. The sick and wounded were crying out for water and in Hook's report on the battle, he said, "We could not bear the cries any longer, and three or four of us jumped over the boxes and ran and fetched some in".
   It is believed they pushed the cart to the boxes, then ran a hose to it, so there was no water shortage.
   The bugler arrives.

Chard: Come with me.

Distant thumping can be heard in the distance as the men position themselves in the redoubt.

Bourne: Get in the redoubt, my lucky lads. Make a move. Come on. Come on.

The soldiers troop in, rifle and bayonet at the ready, whilst the Zulus appear on the hillside, silhouetted against a red sky.

Bourne: Alright lads, take up your positions on the firing step. Keep your heads down.

The men kneel, hidden behind the high stack of mealie bags. The thumping is getting louder as the Zulus approach.

Chard (To bugler):   How old are you, boy?
Bugler: Sir?
Chard: It doesn't matter. You know what to sound?
Bugler: Yes, sir.
Chard: Stay by me.

The Zulus are lining up in formation, determined to try and finally overthrow the shrinking garrison.
   Suddenly the Zulus start singing, which they never did, and start to wave their spears in the air and stamp their feet.
   Chard's men are as quiet as the grave, but he needs to rouse them for one last stand. He walks over to Private Owen.

SCENE 13 - MEN OF HARLECH/FINAL REDOUBT

Chard: Do you think the Welsh can't do better than that, Owen?

Owen: Well they've got a very good bass section, mind, but no top tenors, that's for sure.

Owen hums, getting a song in tune, and starts to sing. "Men of Harlech stop your dreaming, can't you see their spear points gleaming? See their warrior pennants streaming, to this battlefield".

Some other men join in, as Chard goes round ordering all the men to sing. Hitch and Allen are still hard at work opening an ammunition box. The Zulus respond, chanting and banging their spears against their shields.

This is great, stirring viewing, but it never happened and we know there is no Welsh regiment, therefore, no choir. If the 24th had broken into song, it would surely have been their regimental song, "The Warwickshire Lads".

The words were written by David Garrick for the Shakespeare Jubilee Festival at Stratford-On-Avon in 1769, and the music has been adopted as the regimental march.

The song goes as follows:-

Ye Warwickshire lads and ye lasses
See what at our jubilee passes
Come revel away, rejoice and be glad
For the lad of all lads, was a Warwickshire lad
And the lad was a Warwickshire lad
Warwickshire lad! All be glad
For the lad was a Warwickshire lad
(All verses, last 2 lines repeat)

Be proud of the charms of your county
Where nature has lavished her bounty
Where much has been given, and some to be spared
For the bard of all bards was a Warwickshire bard
And the bard was a Warwickshire bard
Warwickshire bard, never paired
For the bard of all bards was a Warwickshire bard

Old Ben, Thomas Otway, John Dryden
And half a score more we take pride in
Of famous Will Congreve we boast to the skill
But the Will of all Wills was a Warwickshire Will
And the Will was a Warwickshire Will
Warwickshire Will! Matchless still!
For the Will of all Wills Was a Warwickshire will

Our Shakespeare compared is to no man
Nor Frenchman, nor Grecian, nor Roman
Their swans are all geese to the Avon's sweet swan
And the man of all men was a Warwickshire man
And the man was a Warwickshire man
Warwickshire man, Avon's swan
For the man of all men was a Warwickshire man

There never was such a creature
Of all she was worth he robbed nature
He took all her smiles, and he took all her grief
And the thief of all thieves was a Warwickshire thief
And the thief was a Warwickshire thief
Warwickshire thief, he's the chief
For the thief of all thieves was a Warwickshire thief

Hope you all sang along to that, but maybe you don't know the tune, never mind.

If you're ever in Warwick, visit St. Mary's church, where every Friday at 9am, midday, 3pm, 6pm, and 9pm, the bells play the, "Warwickshire Lads".

Meanwhile, the Zulus are working themselves into a frenzy, probably a cocktail of drugs and Welsh singing aiding them, and they charge forward as one.

Bromhead: At 100 yards! Volley fire! Present! Fire!

Fierce fighting breaks out on the front barricade, Bromhead using his revolver, with the men in the redoubt hidden from view. Chard approaches the bugler.

Chard: Right, stand by. Lips dry? Now!

The bugler falters as he tries to blow the bugle.

Chard: Spit, boy! Spit!

This time the bugler blows the call to retreat, and the men fall back to the redoubt, making two lines, one standing, the other kneeling. The men in the redoubt now rise, producing three ranks of fire power.

Chard: Redoubt party! Fire!

The Zulus are hit with a volley of tremendous power, as bodies crash to the floor.

Bromhead: Volley by ranks! Front rank, fire!
Chard: Second rank, fire!
Bromhead: Third rank, fire! Front rank, fire!

The orders are repeated, as the Zulus suffer great losses, and are stopped dead in their tracks.

As Chard yells, "Cease firing!", we see scores of dead and wounded Zulus laying right up to the first rank, some writhing in agony.

Work now begins clearing the dead and collecting the weapons, as it seems the garrison has held out against overwhelming odds.

It was while collecting the weapons that Hook had a narrow escape, as he recalled in his account of the battle.

"I was walking up the dry bed of a little stream near the drift with my own rifle in my right shoulder and a bunch of assegais over my left shoulder. Suddenly I came across an unarmed Zulu lying on the ground, apparently dead, but bleeding from the leg. Thinking it strange that a dead man should bleed, I hesitated, and wondered whether I should go on, as other Zulus might be lurking about. But I resumed my task. Just as I was passing, the supposed dead man seized the butt of my rifle and tried to drag it away, the bunch of assegais rattled to earth. The Zulu suddenly released his grasp of the rifle with one hand, and with the other fiercely endeavoured to drag me down. The fight was short and sharp, but it ended by the Zulu being struck in the chest with the butt and knocked to the ground.

The rest was quickly over. After that we were not allowed to go on with our task, except in two's and three's".

Chard kept the men busy as the thatched roof on the storehouse was stripped, the hospital walls pulled down, and shrubs and trees cut down, which they hadn't time to do before the battle.

Bromhead: Three hours and they haven't come back.
Bourne: Mr. Chard, sir. The patrol's come back. The Zulus have gone. All of them.

I remember watching the film for the first time, and was hoping that the Zulus would return, as I didn't want it to end.

Bourne: It's a miracle.
Chard: If it's a miracle, Colour Sergeant, it's a short chamber, boxer – henry. 45 calibre miracle.
Bourne: And a bayonet, sir, with some guts behind it.

How very true that statement is, as there was ferocious hand to hand combat throughout the battle, with the defenders never flinching, and showing nerves of steel.

Bromhead: Fall them in. Call the roll.
Bourne: Sir!
Bromhead: Well, you did it.
Chard: Me?

The men hurriedly form ranks as Bourne begins the roll.

Bourne: Abel?

There is no record of this name.

Abel: Sir.
Bourne: Adams? Adams? Barry?

No answer from Adams which is correct. There was a Private 987 Robert Adams who was a patient in the hospital, and who was killed in action. He is buried in the cemetery at Rorkes Drift.
    There was also a Private 1381 Thomas Barry.

Barry: Sir.
Bourne: Beckett?

True again. Private 135 William Beckett, another patient in the hospital, was killed in action,(see scene 11), and is buried at the battlefield.

Hughes: He's wounded sir.
Thomas: He's dying sir.
Owen: It's sad.
Bourne: Keep your voices down. Byrne?

There is no record of this name.

Bourne: Camp?

True, Private 1181 William Henry Camp.

Camp: Sir.
Bourne: Chick?

True, Private 1332 James Chick, another patient, killed in action and buried at Rorkes Drift.

Bourne: Cole?

There were two Cole's. Private 1459 Robert, and 801 Thomas, who was killed in action. Thomas is buried at Rorkes Drift with the others.

The roll call continues as Chard and Bromhead survey the remains of the burnt out hospital, as the smell of burning flesh hangs in the air.

Chard: Who was left in here?
Bromhead: I don't know.
Chard: They had names, they had faces. They were our men, what do you mean, you don't know?
Bromhead: Chard.
Chard: Alright. Well, you've fought your first action.

This is not true. It was Chard's first action, but Bromhead was posted to South Africa on 2/2/78 and served in the Kaffir War of 1878.

Bromhead: Does everyone feel like this afterwards?
Chard: How do you feel?
Bromhead: Sick.
Chard: Well, you have to be alive to be sick.
Bromhead: You asked me, I told you. There's something else. I feel ashamed. Was that how it was for you? The first time?
Chard: The first time? You think I could stand this butcher's yard more than once?

It was, as we already know, Chard's first action, but he was present at Ulundi, where the Zulus were finally beaten. He took a Zulu shield from Ulundi as a souvenir, which has written on it, "From Ulundi 4th July 1879", and is personally signed by Chard. This can be viewed at the Royal Engineer's museum, Chatham, Kent.

Bromhead: I didn't know.
Chard: I told you, I came up here to build a bridge.

The roll call continues.

Bourne: Fagan?

True. Private 969 John Fagan, killed in action and buried at Rorkes Drift.

Bourne: Green, 459?

There is no record of this name, but he answers.

| Green: | Sir. |
| Bourne: | Hughes? |

Again, no record.

| Hughes: | Excused duty. |

This brings a light hearted moment, and the men laugh.

Bourne:	No comedians, please. Hughes?
Hughes:	Yes, Colour Sergeant.
Bourne:	Say "Sir". Officer on parade.
Hughes:	Sir!
Bourne:	Hayden?

True. Private 1769 Garret Hayden, killed in action and buried with his comrades at the battle site.

| Bourne: | Hitch? Hitch? I saw you. You're alive. |

True. Private 1362 Frederick Hitch, V.C. who has been discussed earlier.

Hitch:	I am? Oh, thanks very much.
Bourne:	Answer the roll. Say "Sir".
Hitch:	Sir!
Bourne:	Alright, now get off to the sickbay where you belong. Hook?

True. Private 1373 Alfred Henry Hook V.C. who we have mentioned in great detail.

| Hook: | Yes, sir, me too. |
| Bourne: | Stay where you are, Hook. |

Hook was hoping to go back to the sickbay too, and the disappointment is etched across his face.

SCENE 14 – THEY'RE SALUTING YOU

About this time, Chard's batman, Robson, came down from the cave he had been hiding in throughout the battle, to rejoin the garrison. Suddenly, a shot is fired by a Zulu hiding in the kraal, which misses his target, and he runs off. Shots were fired at him, which also missed the lucky warrior. Chard was glad that the, "plucky fellow" escaped. Those bullets fired, were part of a massive total of 20,000 rounds spent.

Chard said of the Zulus, " I thought at the time they were going to attack us, but what I know from Zulus, and also of the number we put "Hors De Combat", I do not think so. I think that they came up on the high ground to observe Lord Chelmsford's advance, from there they could see the column long before it came in sight of us".

Bromhead: Well, we haven't done too badly. Hmmm?

Chard is staring into the distance, unaware of what Bromhead is saying, as Bromhead looks up to see what Chard is looking at, and his face drops at the sight.

Bromhead: Oh, my God!

On top of the hill, the Zulus are formed up, just like the first time they appeared in their thousands.

Back in the London cinema, I felt like cheering. The music grows louder and surely all hope for the garrison must be over. The Zulus begin to chant, then stop.

Chard: Adendorff, why have they stopped?

Adendorff: God damn you.
Chard: I want an answer.
Adendorff: Haven't you had enough? Both of you! My god, can't you see it's all over? Your bloody egos don't matter anymore! We're dead.

Bromhead shouts up at the Zulus.

Bromhead: What are you waiting for? Come on! Come on!

Bromhead starts to laugh as the Zulu chanting starts again. The rest of the garrison are quiet, as the men are virtually dead on their feet.

Bromhead: Those bastards! They're taunting us.
Adendorff (laughing):   No. No. You couldn't be more wrong. They're …….. saluting you.

Bromhead laughs out loudly.

Adendorff: They're saluting fellow braves. (Laughing). They're saluting you.

As Chard stares up, the Zulus turn and head away. In the cinema, I'm gutted.

Hitch: Oh, my eye! Oh my eye! Will you look?

The last Zulu, no doubt a leader, turns round and raises both spear and shield, just like the beginning of the film at Islandlwana, then slowly walks back down the hill and out of sight.

The Zulus did reappear on the western slope of the Oskarsberg, but only for a short rest and time to take a little snuff. They did not salute, but headed away back to their homes. As they stopped at the Buffalo river for water, they noticed Chelmsford's column coming to relieve Rorkes Drift. Not wishing an engagement the Zulus turned away, although rumour has it, that the superstitious Zulus, thought they were seeing ghosts from Islandlwana, and were unsettled by the experience.

Chelmsford was about 400 yards away and not prepared for conflict, so he would have been pleased to see his deflated enemy depart.

Back in the camp, Chard found a bottle of beer in the engineer's wagon, which the Zulus had overlooked, and shared it with Bromhead.

Relief came at 8.15am, when Major Cecil Russell of the 12th lancers, rode up with his mounted troops. Chelmsford, with his staff followed shortly afterwards, a much relieved man, seeing the post still standing.

On hearing of Hook's gallantry, Chelmsford demanded to see him. Hook was in his short sleeves, busy again making tea for the sick men, when he was told by Bromhead.

"Wait till I put my coat on", said Hook. "Come as you are, straight away", replied Bromhead.

Chelmsford quizzed Hook about the defence of the hospital and visited the wounded Hitch, promising he would do everything in his power to get him a V.C. which he did.

In the light of the day, the terrible mutilation of the British dead could be seen. Private Hayden, one of the hospital patients, had been stabbed 16 times, his belly cut open in 2 places and part of his cheek cut off. In total, the garrison lost 17 men, 15 dead and 2 mortally wounded, whilst the Zulu dead cannot be accurately recorded. Buried at Rorkes Drift, the official number of Zulu dead is 351, but there would be more casualties in the rocks and caves, with many more dying on the way back home. Plus, all wounded Zulus were finished off by both British and NNC troops. The motive must have been revenge for Islandlwana.

Commandant Hamilton-Browne of the 1/3rd NNC, recorded what happened when his men discovered a large number of wounded and worn out Zulus, in nearby mealie fields.

"My two companies of Zulus with some of my non-coms, and a few of the 24th, quickly drew these fields and killed them with bayonet butt and assegai. It was beastly, but there was nothing else to do. War is war and savage war is the worst of the lot. Moreover our men were worked up to a pitch of fury by the sights they had seen in the morning and the mutilated bodies of the poor fellows laying in front of the burned hospital".

What upset the relief column was the death of 5 band boys at Islandlwana. They had either been tied to wagons by their feet and had their throats cut, or hung on butcher's hooks by their chins, their privates cut off and placed in their mouths. Because of this, boys were never taken on active duty again. Many other bodies were found, disembowelled and decapitated.

Lieutenant-Colonel Crealock's journal entry for 23rd January states, "351 dead and 500 wounded were found", yet no prisoners were taken and no mention is made of the wounded.

The Zulus neither gave or expected quarter, and like the one who attacked Hook, would carry on fighting, even when wounded, to the death.

At least one prisoner was taken by Private James Ashton, after the battle on January 23rd.

He approached Bromhead with the prisoner and asked what he was to do with him. Bromhead, busy at the time, snapped, "Get the hell out of here with him".

Ashton took this literally, and hanged the unfortunate Zulu.

This was confirmed by Lieutenant Smith-Dorrien, who witnessed two Zulus hanging from the gallows he had erected to stretch hides, not Zulu necks.

Ashton, must have been a good soldier, because when he was discharged on 29/3/81, he had served over 21 years.

So the garrison held out, thanks to the bravery of each and every man who stood that day. Their comradeship was solid from the officers down to the non – combatants. The friendship between Bromhead and Hitch being a prime example. Everyone worked for one another, even the wounded, and not once did they flinch when faced with superior odds. Even the early desertion of all those men before the battle did not deter these heroes, who proved once again that the British soldier is the best in the world. Or should that be Welsh or English? I think you know that by now.

93

SCENE 15 – THE ELEVEN V.C.s

Here, as in the beginning, Richard Burton narrates, "In the 100 years since the Victoria Cross was created for valour and extreme courage beyond that expected of a British soldier in face of the enemy, only 1,344 have been awarded. Eleven of these were won by the defender's of the mission station at Rorke's Drift, Natal, January 22nd to the 23rd, 1879".

In the film, the men are digging graves for their fallen comrades as Chard and Bromhead walk over. As Richard Burton reads out the V.C. recipients, Schiess is still hobbling on his crutches, Allen is taking a drink from a water bottle and passes it to Hitch who pours it over his face. Dalton looks on as a body passes on a stretcher and tips his hat. Williams is sat reading, whilst Robert and William Jones sit chatting. Hook is carving his name on a wooden beam with a bloody Zulu spear and Reynolds is still operating on a wounded man.

Bromhead walks over to greet the relief column and finally, Chard surveys the scene and throws a Zulu spear to the ground. Here is the list of the eleven V.C. recipients in film order.

Frederick Scheiss, corporal, Natal Native Contingent.

William Allen, corporal, "B" company, 2nd battalion, 24th foot.

Fred Hitch, private, "B" company, 2nd battalion, 24th foot.

James Langley Dalton, Acting Assistant Commissary, Army Commissariat Department.

612 John Williams, private, "B" company, 2nd battalion, 24th foot.

716 Robert Jones, 593 William Jones, privates, "B" company, 2nd battalion, 24th foot.

Henry Hook, private, "B" company, 2nd battalion, 24th foot.

James Henry Reynolds, Surgeon Major, Army Hospital Corps.

Gonville Bromhead, Lieutenant, "B" company, 2nd battalion of the 24th regiment of foot, South Wales Borderers.

John Rouse Merriott Chard, Lieutenant, Royal Engineer's, officer commanding Rorkes Drift.

Scheiss' real name was Christian Ferdinand, but he liked to be called Frederick, and his name is sometimes spelt Schiess.

612 John Williams, was alias John Williams Fielding as earlier mentioned, and his actual number was 1395.

The facts about the eleven V.C. winners are true, except for the howler regarding Bromhead being with the South Wales Borderers. Why single him out is a mystery because we are supposed to believe it was a Welsh regiment, but I have cleared that matter in Scene 3, in which Bromhead introduces himself to Chard as Bromhead, 24th.

I have given details of some of these heroes earlier, but I am going to go through them all again in the order they appeared in the film.

Corporal Christian Ferdinand Schiess, Natal Native Contingent
Born near Berne in Switzerland, Schiess was a patient in the hospital with a badly blistered foot and was 23 years old at the time.

Arriving in South Africa, he joined the 2nd battalion, 3rd NCC as a corporal. As in the film, he left the hospital to take part in the battle. Having his hat shot off, he sprang onto the barricade and bayoneted the shooter, shot another, then bayoneted a third. He then sustained a gunshot wound to his injured foot, but bravely fought on.

He was the first colonial to be awarded the Victoria Cross, overruling the War Offices law of awarding V.C.'s to British only.

After the war he worked in a telegraph office in Durban, but by 1884 he was destitute and took the offer of a free passage to England onboard HMS Serapis. Unfortunately, he died on the voyage aged 28 years and was buried at sea. Destitute as he was, his V.C. was found on his body, and is now on display in the National Army Museum. There is no record of any photograph of this brave man.

Corporal William Wilson Allen

Born in 1844, Allen attested at York on 27/10/59, aged 15 years 8 months. He joined the regiment at Aldershot on 31/10/59 and served in Mauritius and South Africa. During his early services, he was confined in cells on many occasions, from 1860-1864. He was appointed Lance-Corporal on 18/5/76 and to his present rank on 6/7/77. He rose to Lance-Sergeant on 22/5/78, but was demoted back to corporal on 21/10/78, no doubt due to his bad discipline.

He was awarded a good shooting and judging distance prize in 1878, which would have served him well. He was wounded at Rorkes Drift, with a gunshot through his arm and shoulder, but continued to hand out ammunition, just like in the film, with private Hitch.

He was awarded his V.C. from Queen Victoria at Windsor Castle on 9/12/79. He returned to England on 26/8/79 and died on 12/3/90, aged 46 years. While he was recovering in South Africa, Allen wrote to his wife in a letter supplied by Victorian Voices, dated 4/2/79 saying, "My dear wife, I trust you will feel too thankful to god for having preserved my life, to fret over what might have been a great deal worse. I feel thankful to god for leaving me in the land of the living. Give my respects to your relatives and love to yourself and the children. From your loving husband."

Private Frederick Hitch

Born Edmonton, London, on 28/11/56. A bricklayer's labourer, he attested at Westminster Police Court on 7/3/77, aged 20 years 3 months. Posted to 2/24th on 11/5/77, he was seriously wounded in the defence of Rorkes Drift, with a gunshot shattering his shoulder blade. He was invalided from the service on 25/8/79 after receiving his V.C. from Queen Victoria at Netley on 12/8/79.

He started work as a commissionaire at the Royal Services Institute in Whitehall, from where he got his V.C. stolen from his coat. King Edward V11 ordered a replacement, which was presented to him in 1908.

Later, he became a cab driver whilst living in Chiswick, where he died on 7/1/13. He was buried at St. Nicholas Church, Old Chiswick on 11/1/13.

James Langley Dalton, Commissariat

Dalton was the man who persuaded Chard and Bromhead that it was too dangerous to attempt a retreat, far better to stay and fortify their position. He also took a very active role throughout the battle, even when wounded, which earned him his V.C.

He was born in the early 1830's and worked as a printer's apprentice, before enlisting into the 85th (Shropshire) Regiment at Victoria, London on 20/11/49, giving his age as 17 years 11 months.

By 1855 he had reached the rank of Sergeant and in 1858 he sailed to the Cape Of Good Hope and was engaged in a number of frontier disputes. In March 1862 after returning to England, he transferred into Commissariat Corps. He was promoted to Colour Sergeant on 1/6/63 and in 1870 transferred to the Army Service Corps, with promotion to Staff Sergeant. He received his discharge on 20/11/71 after nearly 22 years service.

Sailing back to South Africa, he was employed on Commissariat duties at the start of the Ninth Cape Frontier War in 1877.

With the invasion of Zululand on the horizon, he moved to Natal with Louis Byrne, and arrived at Rorkes Drift on 1/1/79.

His severe wounds took six months for him to recover fully, and he was then appointed Senior Commissariat Officer at Fort Napier, Pietermaritzburg. Promoted to Assistant Commissary on 13/12/79, he sailed back to England and into obscurity.

He did return to South Africa and was part owner of the Little Bess Gold Mine. He was taken ill and died on 7/1/87 and is buried in Russell Road Catholic Cemetery, Port Elizabeth. On 26/9/1986 his medal's were auctioned at Spink and Son in London, for which the Royal Corps of Transport paid £62,000.

Private John Williams (Alias Fielding)

Born at Abergavenny, Monmouthshire, on 24/5/57, and attested at Monmouth on 22/5/77. He ran away from home and used his second christian name to avoid being traced. Posted to 2/24th on 3/8/77, he served in South Africa and India.

Awarded his V.C. for his part in the defence of the hospital and was presented with it by Major- General Anderson at Gibraltar on 1/3/80.

After serving in India, he returned to England in October, 1883 and transferred to the Army Reserve, where he was discharged on 22/5/93. He worked on the civilian staff at the Regimental Depot in Brecon for many years, before retiring on 26/5/20. In 1932 he was taken ill and died on 25/11/32. He is buried at St. Michael's Churchyard, Llantarnam.

Private Robert Jones

Born at Penrose, Raglan, Monmouth and attested at Monmouth on 10/1/76 aged 18 years 5 months.

Posted to 2/24th on 28/1/76 and served in South Africa, Gibraltar and India.

Slightly wounded in the defence of the hospital and received his V.C. from Sir Garnet Wolseley at Utrecht on 11/9/79. He was one of the men who tried in vain to get Sergeant Maxfield out of the burning hospital.

Served at the Regimental Depot and Army Reserve, and discharged on 26/1/88. He died on 6/9/98 and is buried at Peterchurch, Hereford.

Private William Jones

Born at Evesham, Worcester (not Welsh), and attested at Birmingham on 21/12/58, aged 19 years.

Served in Mauritius, East Indies and South Africa. Promoted corporal 1/9/59, demoted 4/9/60, he re-engaged at Rangoon on 10/1/68 to complete 21 years service.

Awarded his V.C. for his part in the hospital fight and received his decoration from Queen Victoria at Windsor Castle on 13/1/80. On 3/9/79 he was examined by a medical board who found him to be suffering from chronic rheumatism. He was invalided to England, where at Netley he was discharged on 2/2/80.

He was forced to sell his V.C. around 1892 when out of work and he died at Ardwick, Manchester on 15/4/13. He was buried on 21/4/13 in a public grave at Phillip Park Cemetery, (Bradford Ward), Manchester. A stone headstone has been erected which says, "To the memory of Private 593 William Jones V.C. "B" coy. 2/24th regt. of foot. Awarded the Victoria Cross for gallantry at the defence of the mission at Rorkes Drift, Natal Province, South Africa, 22nd/23rd January 1879. Died Manchester 15th April 1913 aged 73 years".

Private Alfred Henry Hook

Born at Churcham, Gloucestershire, in May 1850 and attested at Monmouth on 13/3/77. He was a farm labourer by trade, who enlisted as the result of a fore-closure on a mortgage. Posted to 2/24th on 11/5/77 and served in "B" company.

Slightly wounded whilst defending the hospital, he was awarded his V.C. by Sir Garnet Wolseley at Rorkes Drift on 3/8/79.

He purchased his discharge for £18 on 25/6/80 and on returning home, found his property sold and his wife, who believed him dead, had re-married. Moving to London, he began work as a labourer at the British Museum, later becoming cloak room attendant. He married on 10/4/97 and despite bad health, served for many years as a sergeant in the 1st Vol. Battalion, Royal Fusiliers. He retired due to bad health on 31/12/04 and died on his return to Gloucester of pulmonary tuberculosis on 12/3/05.

He was buried in the churchyard at Churcham.

Surgeon James Henry Reynolds

He arrived in South Africa in 1875 after serving in the Tropics for many years. The casualties were not taken to Reynolds, operating in Witt's house like in the film, but were treated in a makeshift redoubt in front of the storehouse. He was promoted to Surgeon Major with effect from 23/1/79 and stayed 'til the final battle at Ulundi.

Lord Wolseley presented him with his V.C. at St. Paul's in Zululand on 16/7/79, which is held by the Royal Army Medical Corps Museum, near Guildford.

He died in 1932 aged 88 years and was buried at Kensal Green, London.

On the day after the battle he said, "I am glad to say that the men of AHC behaved splendidly".

Lieutenant Gonville Bromhead

Born on 29/8/45 at Versailles, France, he was the 3rd son of Edmund De Gonville Bromhead, 3rd Baronet, and his wife Judith Christine Cahill.

The family home was at Thurlby Hall in Newark. He joined the 24th as an ensign, by purchase, on 20/4/67, and promoted Lieutenant on 28/10/71.

Served in the Kaffir War in 1878 and commanded "B" company 2nd/24th foot at Rorkes Drift.

Promoted Captain and Brevet-Major on 23/1/79, Major on 4/4/83, then posted from South Africa to Gibraltar, where he served until March 1881. Retuning home in 1882 for a short while, he sailed from Portsmouth on 2/1/83 to join the 2nd South Wales Borderers, (yes, they do get a mention at the correct time), in India. He died of enteric fever on 9/2/91, aged 46 years, at camp Dabhaura, Allahabad.

A revolver was presented to him by the tenants of Thurlby Hall and the people of Lincoln gave him a sword. Queen Victoria also gave him a personal photograph of herself. He left all these belongings, along with his V.C. to his brother, Colonel Charles J. Bromhead and left no written report regarding Rorkes Drift.

Lieutenant John Rouse Merriott Chard

Born on 21/12/47 at Boxhill, near Plymouth, he entered the Royal Military Academy at Woolwich, which he struggled to pass.

Commissioned on 14/7/68, and after two more years of training with the Royal Engineer's at Chatham, he was posted to Bermuda in October 1870.

Returning to England for his father's funeral in 1874, he was then posted to Malta to construct the island's sea defences. Posted back to England in 1876, he held a number of small positions before being posted to the 5th Company Royal Engineer's at Aldershot.

He sailed to South Africa on 2/12/78 arriving at Durban on 5/1/79, and was detailed to assist on the river crossing at Rorkes Drift, arriving on January 19.

After the battle, he assisted with the construction of a stone fort at the site, and after a bout of fever, rejoined 5th company, where he was present at the last Zulu War battle at Ulundi on July 4.

Later on he was found to have cancer of the mouth, and in November 1896, had an operation in Edinburgh to try and cure it. It was whilst he was recovering that he was made Colonel on 8/1/97.

He needed a second operation in March 1897, where the surgeons removed part of his tongue, but remarkably he could still converse to a high level.

Unfortunately, on a visit to Edinburgh in August 1897, he was told the cancer was terminal. He went to visit his younger brother, the Rev. Charles E. Chard at Hatch Beauchamp, Taunton and gracefully accepted his fate. He died on 1/11/97, and it says a great deal of this man, that Queen Victoria, as recently as 30/10/97, had enquired about his health.

Messages of sympathy were received by Rev. Chard from HRH The Duke Of Connaught, who attended the Royal Academy at Woolwich with Chard and Lord Chelmsford, commander of the Anglo-Zulu War.

He was buried on 5/11/97 at his brother's church, The Parish Church Of St. John The Baptist at Hatch Beauchamp.

Queen Victoria sent a wreath of laurel leaves tied with long streamers of white satin. The tribute bore a card in her majesty's own handwriting saying, "A mark of admiration and regard for a brave soldier. From his sovereign, Victoria R.I."

The queen's wreath lay for many years under the Chard Memorial Window, which was installed in 1899. The polished oak coffin, with brass mountings, bore the inscription, "John R.M. Chard, born 21st December 1847 died 1st November 1897".

In due course a headstone was placed on the grave, which was replaced by the present one some years later. It consists of a cross on a three tiered plinth, surrounded by a rail and all in rose coloured marble. It reads, "In memoriam, Col. J.R.M. Chard, VC, RE. The hero of Rorkes Drift. Born 21st Dec. 1847. Died 1st Nov. 1897. Son of W.W.Chard of Pathe, Somerset and Mount Tamar, Devon."

SCENE 16 - END CREDITS

Chard sticks a Zulu shield into the ground as "Men of Harlech" plays in the background.

This film, a Diamond Films Production, was filmed in Natal, South Africa and Twickenham Film Studios, England.

It had it's premiere in the UK on 22/1/64 and was released on 17/6/64. It was released again in London on 3/2/1972, as a 70mm version.

The film lasts approximately 133 minutes, of which I enjoyed every minute.

Credits

Director	Cy Endfield
Produced by	Cy Endfield/Stanley Baker
Associate Producer	Basil Keys
Production Manager	John D. Merriman
Art Director	Earnest Archer
Editor	John Jympson
2nd Unit Director	Bob Porter
Director Of Photography	Stephen Dade, BSC
Screenplay by	John Prebble/Cy Endfield
From an original story by	John Prebble
Music composed and conducted by	John Barry
Make-up created by	Charles Parker
Wardrobe Supervisor	Arthur Newman

CASUALTIES

The total number of men killed in the battle was 15, plus 2 mortally wounded as listed.

Killed - Pte. William Horrigan, Pte. James Jenkins, Pte. Edward Nicholas, Sgt. Robert Maxfield, Pte. Robert Adams, Pte. James Chick, Pte. Thomas Cole, Pte. John Fagan, Pte. Garret Hayden, Pte. John Scanlon, Pte. Joseph Williams, Louis Byrne, Trooper Hunter, Corp. Anderson, Unknown native of NNC.

Mortally wounded - Pte. William Beckett and L/Sgt. Thomas Williams.